Black Feminist
Archaeology

*For Egun, my ancestors, and the Old Ones.
Those whose names are known and those whose
names have been forgotten. Thank you for giving me
the strength to pull the words together to
tell your story…*

Black Feminist Archaeology

Whitney Battle-Baptiste

Routledge
Taylor & Francis Group

LONDON AND NEW YORK

First published 2011 by Left Coast Press, Inc.

Published 2016 by Routledge
2 Park Square, Milton Park, Abingdon, Oxon OX14 4RN
711 Third Avenue, New York, NY 10017, USA

Routledge is an imprint of the Taylor & Francis Group, an informa business

Library of Congress Cataloging-in-Publication Data

Battle-Baptiste, Whitney.
  Black feminist archaeology / Whitney Battle-Baptiste.
    p. cm.
  Includes bibliographical references.
  ISBN 978-1-59874-378-4 (hardcover : alk. paper)—ISBN 978-1-59874-379-1
(pbk.   )—ISBN 978-1-59874-665-5 (electronic)
1. African American women–History. 2. African Americans–Antiquities. 3. Feminist archaeology–United States. 4. African American feminists. 5. Historic sites–United States. 6. Archaeology and history–United States. 7. Social archaeology–United States. I. Title.
  E185.86.B3758 2011
  930.1082–dc23

                            2011017041

  ISBN 978-1-59874-378-4 hardcover
  ISBN 978-1-59874-379-1 paperback

Contents

List of Illustrations. 6

Foreword by Maria Franklin. 7

Acknowledgments 11

Introduction: Understanding a Black Feminist Framework. 19

Chapter I.   Constructing a Black Feminist Framework. 33

Chapter II.   The Hermitage. 73

Chapter III.   Revisiting Excavations at Lucy Foster's
                Homestead. 109

Chapter IV.   The Burghardt Women and the
                W. E. B. Du Bois Boyhood Homesite. 135

Chapter V.   Moving Mountains and Liberating
                Dialogues 163

References 173

Index. 191

About the Author. 199

Illustrations

Figures

Figure 1.1: African American women excavating at
Irene Mound. 69

Figure 2.1: An engraving of the Hermitage Mansion
as it appeared in the 1830s. 79

Figure 2.2: Map of Hermitage archaeological areas
investigated between 1989 and 2000. 81

Figure 2.3: Map of First Hermitage archaeology. 84

Figure 2.4: Close up picture of Feature 820, the cooking pit. 103

Figure 2.5: Hannah Jackson, also known as "Old Hannah,"
and two great-grandchildren. 105

Figure 3.1: Plan of Lucy Foster Homestead. 121

Figure 3.2: Items from the Lucy Foster Homesite. 128

Figure 3.3: One of several transfer printed pearlware teacups. . . . 129

Figure 4.1: "House of the Black Burghardts." 139

Figure 4.2: Mary Burghardt Du Bois and W. E. B. Du Bois
as an infant. 140

Figure 4.3: An assortment of artifacts from the
W. E. B. Du Bois Boyhood Homesite. 156

Figure 4.4: Signage of current trail at Du Bois Boyhood
Homesite. 160

Tables

Table 3.1. Lucy Foster's Annual Dole from the Fund
for Relief of Indigent Persons in the
South Parish Congregational Church. 117

Table 3.2. Lucy Foster's Chronology. 123

Foreword

I can't think of another work written by a scholar that starts with as revealing an assertion as, "I begin this journey with a moment of honesty." Moreover, taking the plunge into the realm of self-revelation (in so public a manner, no less) is rare for an archaeologist. We generally prefer the comfort of a couch cushioned by distance and objectivity. Yet the journey that Battle-Baptiste leads us through is not only one that brings into focus her motivations, objectives, and importantly, her life history, it is one that encourages each of us to examine our own in the pursuit and production of knowledge. This is not an exercise in self-reflectivity that leaves us wondering about its relevance to anything else, let alone archaeology. It is a positioning, a standpoint, if you will, that situates Battle-Baptiste within a politics of black feminism, a legacy of black vindicationist scholarship, a history of black struggle and resistance, and a range of transformative practices in archaeology. Yet she envisions this space as one that is open to all of those who seek to challenge inequality along its many fronts, in her claims that, "I did not write a book to push for a theoretical agenda that excludes anyone. I write for an audience that is ready to hear about how race, gender and class complicate the field of archaeology and make it relevant to the larger world."

Critical self-reflection, politics, and alternative forms of writing are not new to archaeology, especially within feminist and social archaeologies. Yet few have ventured to relate their missteps, anxieties, hopes, anger, intellectual growth, and passion with respect to archaeology and their relationship to it as the author has done here. Thus, while archaeologists will be familiar with the topics (households, landscape, class, women's labor and consumer practices, etc.), Battle-Baptiste's black feminist theorizing brings us onto less-traveled terrain for the discipline. She maintains an active presence in the text as she takes us through her process of forming questions about the past, and questioning the canon as she seeks an alternative, more inclusive and politically responsible way to engage with the past. Battle-Baptiste relies as much on black women's literary traditions as she does the usual academic scholarship in constructing her narrative, which is rooted to her veneration of family and ancestral matriarchs. People are highlighted over artifacts within these pages, gently reminding us what our research is supposed to be about. The mystifying language of archaeology is replaced by a welcoming one of accessibility, a voice that seeks a much broader audience defined by the author as "my elders, my peers, my children and my community." Thus, while Battle-Baptiste reaches back to recover the past, she also reaches out with the goal of placing her work in the hands of those beyond the spheres of academe and the profession.

The journey that Battle-Baptiste maps for us traverses individual and group histories, a range of geographical spaces and eras, and her own personal memories. She takes us from the Hermitage Plantation during her formative years as an archaeologist, to the walls of her campus office at UMass, and eventually to the site of the W.E.B. DuBois childhood home, with other destinations of import along the way. It is a journey that underscores the relationship between the past and present, and the positive role that positionality can play in the research process. Ultimately, this journey is one of recovery and healing. It compels us to take seriously the omissions of our craft in writing narratives that deny the presence of women, let alone their contributions as scholars and historical agents.

Reading this book brought back memories of attending my first Society for American Archaeology annual meeting in the early 1990s.

As far as I could tell (and, trust me, I looked), I was not only the sole black woman in attendance, I was the only person of African descent. That this book even exists, therefore, is a wonder to me. Nonetheless, I certainly empathized with Battle-Baptiste when she recalled her frustration as a black woman of being rendered invisible, and thus unheard: "There were many moments when I was screaming at the top of my lungs to look around and realize that no one was listening." How many out there have raised their voices only to be tuned out because of their class, race, sexuality, gender, age, nationality, religion, and so on? So open up your ears, folks, and listen. The message is well worth it. Inspired by the black women that she hails herein, those who sung the blues, fought to keep their families together and their dignities intact, and those who still struggle against tremendous odds, Battle-Baptiste has wielded her keyboard in bringing awareness to the life stories of those who have too long walked in the shadows and invites us to bear witness to them. In doing so, she provides another crucial perspective to the growing literature on the potentials for transforming archaeological practice and theory, and the rationales for why this is necessary.

Maria Franklin

Acknowledgments

There are so many people that I would like to thank. They came into my life at different moments, in different places, and some I have known for a lifetime. Writing it has allowed me to understand that this project was not a solo effort. I would like to begin with thanking my family (family in many forms). My mother, Andrea Battle, for her love, support and encouragement in even the darkest moments of the writing process and for helping during those needy moments and reading countless drafts, and believing it would all come together. To my father, C. Whitaker Battle, for your love and support throughout the years; may we continue to build on what we already have (over the next thirty plus years). To my second mother, Gail Bell-Baptiste, for the love, advice and motivating words: they always helped me put things in perspective and kept me going even in the most tired of moments. To one of my other mothers, Lucy Atwood, for all the years of love and support. I cherish our relationship and am so happy that you will always be a part of my life and family. To my great-aunt Theda and the best cousins a woman could have: Sandy Robertson; Pamela, Rodney and Helen George; Robert, Linda and Eric Mitchell. For my sister for life, Ernestine Christian-Fitzpatrick, for keeping up with me even when I disappear for long spans of time. I know you are always my backup whenever I need you! To my "prima" extraordinaire, Wanda Ramos Rodriguez; so glad to always have you in my life, no matter how far the distance between us. To Angelica Castro and Gilbert McCauley, for being there as friends, family, and comrades in the struggle to raise wonderful children, and for your inspiration and love always. To the Ulysse and Baptiste families, for opening their arms and hearts to me and making me feel like an instant member of the family. To Aunt Bridget Togans, for taking my phone calls at the most interesting of moments and listening to a variety of problems, blessings and craziness. To my godparents, Oseye Mchawi and Isoke Nia Kierstedt. To my Iyalosa, for your guidance and support, helping me to grow as a person on many levels; your lessons will be with me forever; and my Ojubona, thank you for your patience, laughter and dedication to all that I decide to do. I know no matter what, through a rainstorm or blizzard, you are there with things to grow on. To my Oba, R. Senemeh Burke, for giving me the tools to work with, the path to travel, and the ability to look back and see new meanings for each lesson and story you have told me. To my other godmother, Stephanie Weaver, for your quiet talks and comfortable conversation; each time I sit with you I learn something that takes me one step further in life. To my "Auntie Twin," K. "Iya Koko" Zauditu-Selassie, for showing me that this can be done with the ancestors by our side. You taught me how to not be afraid to write in a way that is liberating for more than just myself. To Sauda Smith, my sister of the white cloth, for your strength, conviction and beauty. I often take my cues from those who have done it with so much grace, and you are one of those! To my entire Ile Ase family, E Se O! (thank you), Joan Morgan, Jude and Tiffany Eugene, Carolyn Jones, Ebony Johnson, Dwana Smallwood, Kiani, Akissi and Barbara Britton, Mandisa Mchawi, Zuwena Mchawi and Cedrick Smith, Sauda Coulter, Amethyst St. Thomas, Lumumba Bandele, Kofi Bernard, Amma McKen, Ololriwaa Amma, Omowale Kierstedt, the Egbe Omo Obatala, Felix Sanabria, Alex Spencer, Junior Bermudez, Gregg Harrison, Raquel Cepeda, Shani Dotts, Imani Johnson, Lorraine Melendez, and my closest friend in the academic game, Tanya Mears, one of the best historians I have ever known.

To my life-long mentors, Maria Franklin and Edmund T. Gordon; Maria, I don't know how to say thank you for all that you have given me over the years. When you first met me, I was rough around the edges, yet you never gave up on me and pulled me through to the other side of this thing we call the academy. Without you, my skills would be dull and my thoughts left unexpressed. To Ted, as a mentor and friend, I value every lesson you have taught me over the years. From teaching, to politics, to not being afraid to speak the truth. Now I honestly believe that it was more than luck that got me to where I am today and will prepare me for the future. To the other members of my dissertation committee, James Denbow, Samuel Wilson, Helena Woodard, thank you for believing in me and making my dissertation experience one to grow on and not one to tear me down. Lastly, thank you to my unofficial mentor for life, Toyin Falola, for all of your words, pushing and motivation that allowed me to see the writer within.

I would like to thank all of the people that helped me during my time at the Hermitage Museum. I learned many lessons at the home of Andrew Jackson, living in middle Tennessee for three months out of every year (for six years) changed me in many ways. To Larry McKee, former Director of Archaeology, Marsha Mullin, Head Curator at the museum, and Tony Guzzi, for their friendship and support and ability to always have the answer to any question, no matter how obscure. To my colleagues that were also a part of my archaeological experience, Brian Thomas, Jillian Galle, Steven Kidd, Nik Ribianzsky, Sarah Mullin, Elizabeth Kellar-DeCorse (former Director of Archaeology), Anna Naruta, Allison Manfra McGovern, Leomie Willoughby-Ellis, Robbie Jones, James Vaughn, and especially to Jennifer Allen Woody, who volunteered hours of her summers to help me process and catalog thousands of artifacts—thank you! And to my lasting relationships with community members such as Constance Bradley, Dorothy Haskins, members of Stateland Baptist Church and Scott's Hallow AME Zion Church.

To my academic friends and colleagues that were there in the early days and have at times inspired me to keep doing better. Saheed Adejumobi, thank you for giving me Fela; now, like you I do my best work with his music in my ears. To Keisha Khan-Perry, Vania Cardosa and Scott Head, Jafari Sinclaire Allen and Philip Alexander, Apen Ruiz, Linta Varghese, Maribel Garcia, Junaid Rana, Peggy Brunache, Paula Saunders, Juliet Hooker, Kia Lilly Caldwell, Shaka McGlotten, Juliet Walker, Jemima Pierre, Joao Vargas, Charles Hale, Lisa Sanchez-Gonzalez, and Manolo Callahan.

For the Cornell years, thank you to Robert Harris for allowing me to have a wonderful transition from graduate student to faculty during my Provost's postdoctoral fellowship. To Salah Hassan, the late Don Ohadike (and his children Sandra, Ophelia and James), James Turner, Ali Mazrui, Mwalimu Abdul Nanji, N'Dri Assie-Lumumba, and one of my favorite Yoruba teachers ever—Adeolu Ademoyo. To Sherene Baugher, for helping to navigate through my transition and helping me publish over and over again. To my "sista doctas" Quinetta Roberson, Audra Simpson, Sherry Martin, Hortense Spillers, and Viranjini Munasinghe. Most of all I must thank my "intellectual auntie," Michele Wallace. Through you, I learned so much about myself, the struggle of Black women and the power of writing in our own voices. I appreciate the two years we spent in the hills of Ithaca together as colleagues and friends. I owe my Black feminist identity to you; you gave me my wings and I plan to fly as far as they will take me. To my sorority sisters of Omicron Nu Omega in Ithaca, New York, Patricia Hairston, Peggy Odom-Reed, Traevena Byrd, Millicent Clarke-Maynard, DiOnetta Jones, Lashanda Korley, Marchel Phillips, Lisa Harris Roberts, and Lauren Harris.

At the University of Massachusetts Amherst, I want to acknowledge the incredible support of the College of Social and Behavioral Sciences, especially my deans, Janet Rifkin and Robert Feldman. They have provided support for travel, research, course development and an open ear to the needs of junior faculty. To the amazing Anthropology Department and my chair, Elizabeth Chilton, who from my arrival at UMass always encouraged me to do what seemed impossible. Thank you for always being honest and believing that this book project would see completion. To my friend and mentor Bob Paynter, thank you for believing in me from the first time you saw me present a passionate, yet completely awful conference paper on the Abeil Smith School in Boston. I value your unwavering support throughout my career. Let us take this Du Bois site to the next level together! To my peer mentor, Krista Harper, whose advice and love has seen me through first year jitters, writing insecurities and two pregnancies. To my many incredible colleagues, Amanda Walker Johnson, Michael Sugerman, H. Martin Wobst, Brian Jones, Mitch Mulholland, Julie Hemment, Art Keene, Betsy Krause, Jackie Urla, Lynnette Leidy Sievert, Laurie Godfrey, Brigitte Holt, Ventura Perez, Neil Silberman, Ralph Faulkingham, H. Enoch Page, Jane Anderson and Jean Forward. To my dedicated and brilliant graduate students, Anthony Martin and Honora Sullivan-Chin; thank you and here's to you making an impact on the world as well. To other students whose work continues to inspire me in so many ways, Chris Douyard, Kamela Heyward-Rotimi, Roderick Anderson, Julie Skogsbergh Pimentel, Quentin Lewis, Evelyn Jeffers, Heidi Bauer-Clapp, Broughton Anderson, Robin Gray, Meg Maccini, and Julie Woods. A special thank you to Donna Moody, whose support has been unwavering, and whose knowledge has brought me back to my Eastern Cherokee roots; thank you for giving me back my Old Ones. At the UMass Du Bois Center, Jay Schafer, Director of Libraries; Carol Connare, Director of Development for UMass Libraries; (former Managing Director) Maurice Hobson; Brooks Fitch, Director of Development for the UMass Du Bois Center; Rob Cox (Acting Director of the UMass Du Bois Center); William Strickland; Amilcar Shabazz (Chair of the W. E. B. Du Bois Department of Afro-American Studies); David Glassberg; Dave Hart and all the members of the Du Bois Center Steering Committee. To my support network at the UMass and the five college consortium, Five College Inc., Five College African Studies/ African Scholars Program, Center for Crossroads in the Study of the Americas (CISA), Demetria Shabazz, Esther Terry, Mari Casteneda, Agustine Lao-Montes, Joye

Bowman, John Higginson, Martha Fuentes-Bautista, John H. Bracy, Jr., Karen Y. Morrison, Joya Misra, Wenona Rymond-Richmond, Enobong Hannah Branch, Melissa Wooten, José A. Hernandez, Sonia Alvarez, Priscilla Page, Alexandrina Deschamps, Mwangi wa Githinji, Riché Barnes, and Renee Brodie.

My friends in the Berkshires, the Friends of the Du Bois Boyhood Homesite, Rachel Fletcher, Wray Gunn and Cora Gunn Portnoff, Elaine Gunn, Bernard Drew, Frances Jones-Sneed and the members of the Upper Housatonic African American Heritage Trail Steering Committee.

Barbara Brown of the Lawrence Historical Society for helping me to know the real story of Lucy Foster, and Gene Winter of the Massachusetts Archaeological Society for the openness and incredible information about archaeology of the time and region. To Linda Bluestain of the Robert S. Peabody Archaeological Museum at Phillips Academy, for helping me to get to know about the collection and the life of Adelaide Bullen. And James Batchelder and the staff and volunteers at the Andover Historical Society in Andover, Massachusetts, for all of their help as well.

To my archaeology and anthropology colleagues across the nation from whom I have learned so much: Laurie Wilkie, Anna Agbe-Davies, Irma McClaurin, Johnetta B. Cole, Ywone Edwards-Ingram, Cheryl LaRoche, Peter Schmidt, Michael Blakey, Marley R. Brown III, Fred McGhee, Fred Smith, Joanne Bowen, Terry Weik, Stephen Pendery, Steven Brighton, Stephen Mrozowski, Mary Beaudry, Suzanne Spencer-Wood, Akin Ogundiran, Paul Mullins, Kimberly Eison Simmons, Chris Fennell, Joan Gero, Gina Ulysse and Christopher Matthews.

I would like to say a special thank you to my extraordinary publisher, Mitch Allen, and everyone at Left Coast. This book was a long time coming! Your patience, faith and strategic nudging made this project a reality. Here's to a long lasting relationship so I can get all of these books out of my head.

Finally, to my children Ayotide and Ololara, thank you for being such bright and shining stars in my life. Through you I see the future and it looks great! Thanks for understanding that "Mommy has to go write" means I will always be home in time to tuck you in. And most of all, to my phenomenal husband, Trevor Armon Baptiste, words cannot express my gratitude for all that you have helped me through with this book. The process, the stress of writing and finishing, keeping all straight on the home front when I disappeared into writing land, and still showing me so much love and patience. Without you I would not understand what happiness or accomplishment feels like. Thank you!

Understanding a
Black Feminist Framework

My great-grandmama told my grandmama the part she lived through that my grandmama didn't live through and my grandmama told my mama what they both lived through and my mama told me what they all lived through and we were suppose to pass it down like that from generation to generation so we'd never forget. Even though they'd burned everything to play like it didn't never happen. Yeah, and where's the next generation?

Gayl Jones, *Corregidora*

We exist as women who are Black, who are feminists, each stranded for the moment, working independently because there is not yet an environment in this society remotely congenial to our struggle—because, being on the bottom, we would have to do what no one else has done: we would have to fight the world.

Wallace 1975: 2

The Journey

I begin this journey with a moment of honesty. I am writing this book with an agenda. I want to present the components of a methodological tool kit that will enable Americanist archaeologists to analyze issues of race, class, and gender in the field of archaeological practice. I am also pushing for the inclusion of this framework across the disciplinary threshold and emphasize how this methodology can be useful to fields such as history, literature, African and African American studies, Africana and African Diaspora studies, critical race, political science, and beyond. This book should be used to open a dialogue that encourages a wider understanding of the intersectionality of race, class and gender in the African American past through the lens of material studies.

This book is written in a personal way. There are both scholarly and narrative elements intertwined throughout the text. I write this book for my colleagues, my peers, my elders and my children. I have often wanted to read a book about archaeology that I could share with anyone I met; however, it is rare that archaeology can serve all these purposes (for exceptions see Wilkie 2003, Franklin 1997a, Mullins 1999, Little 2007, Saitta 2007, Yentsh 1994). This need to share the value of contemporary post-contact archaeology is a testament to how passionate I am about this field, this work, and this research. I want this book to be used in the classroom, the community center, and the household.

To be an archaeologist at this moment comes with an enormous responsibility; there are competing expectations and conflicting loyalties. We as practitioners have to understand our position in the larger contemporary world. Activism as a recognized aspect of Americanist archaeology translates into an inherently political field that often has a direct impact on the communities we are attempting to serve and communicate with (Potter 1994, LaRoche & Blakey 1999, Saita 2007, Shackel 2010). Taking on this role is not easy; it is abundantly clear that we can no longer simply begin and end with the artifact and trust that our work will speak for itself. The artifact is an essential element, but as it was during its lifetime, it can be used, discarded and forgotten by living people. Archaeologists are using the visual aspects of material and the collaborative relationship with descendant communities and other stakeholders to create complex and exciting research models.

As an archaeologist of African descent, I feel an additional responsibility to this engaged methodological approach to the material past. For I am accountable to my elders, the local community where a site is located, my university colleagues, my academic peers and the generations to come. As the years go by I recognize that my audience has grown beyond museum administrators, a dissertation committee, or even colleagues in the anthropology department at the University of Massachusetts Amherst. This added responsibility is tremendous and at times trying, especially when faced with colleagues and friends who often do not understand the complexities of being in such a position. These years have also come with valuable lessons that continue to shape my approach to research. I have learned that some of the key stakeholders that I think about when I write and interpret rarely attend the professional conferences where I present papers; these stakeholders rarely subscribe to the journals that I contribute articles to; and lastly those whom I write about are no longer here to tell me if I am getting it right. However, I continue to seek a balance to provide opportunities for the larger African-descendant community, the archaeological community, and academics from across disciplines to use my work and one day see the value of addressing both race and gender in a more textured understanding of the history of African America.

I want to make it clear that I have never claimed that my life experiences or subject position make my opinions more valid or significant than colleagues that do not share my racialized or gendered identity. Instead, I wish to highlight that my identity often urges me to ask different questions, see from different perspectives, and maintain an ongoing and honest dialogue with my colleagues and various stakeholders (Battle-Baptiste 2007b). In reality, my identity as an archaeologist of African descent can at times be somewhat contradictory. For example, is it plausible to consider myself a part of the larger descendant community by birthright and simultaneously to be a member of the academy or research team that is interpreting a site? There are pros and cons to this contradiction; however, I continue to see this precarious position as a vehicle for me to discuss complex topics such as race, gender and class in unique and challenging ways (Orser 1998b, Harrison 1999, Matthews 1997, Bolles 2001). This book is an effort to see how this position has the potential for creating a new direction in the overall conversation within African Diaspora archeology.

The Meaning of "Race"

What does it mean to be of African descent in America? What does it mean to agree that "Race" is a social construct and not a biological fact (AAA Statement on Race 1998)? What does it mean to live an existence where the direct effects of racism are still a part of the everyday? I would like to ask the reader to now apply these queries to real life and how the answers to these questions are a direct influence on how you may think about this country's historical past. There are no right answers, no set patterns. Each individual will answer these questions in a multitude of ways that can vary for many reasons. Our individual and collective experiences temper how we view the past and alter how we see ourselves in the present. Right at the center of all of this interpretive power is the idea of how we see Race in the past, the present and future, as well as the consideration of the very real consequences that may follow our analyses. For Americanist archaeologists the period of innocence has passed. Archaeologist Paul Mullins asserts that at this moment "we cannot continue to operate out of ignorance or think that the work we do is just going to solve a problem without naming it, the mere act of doing diasporan archaeology is not going to assuage anyone of some deep seated guilt they may bring to the table" (Mullins 2008). There must be a proactive approach to the archaeology of captive African people.

It is safe to say that there are many things that post-contact archaeology gets wrong on a regular basis—and in this I include myself (Battle-Baptiste 2007b, 2010b). However, these starts and stops are a part of how a discipline develops, shifts, and moves forward. These flaws are the stuff that keeps the discipline honest and fluid in nature and context (Franklin 2001, Orser 1998b). My hope is that one day more archaeologists will openly discuss our personal influences, the impact of our backgrounds and experiences, and how these factors could be assets if added to a collective conversation rather than words suspended in the isolating landscape of individual self reflexivity (for examples see Blakey 1997, McDavid 1995, Patten 1997, Galle & Young 2004). We often, by habit or practice, want to highlight the positives, the basics of inquiry and always showcase our artifact "goodies," without showing any aspect of our indecision in how we originally thought we were going to excavate a site or the confusion we experience as the research questions and agenda change on a daily basis. I have gained so much from casual conversations with archaeologists about the dirty details of the everyday ups and downs of real archaeology. These are aspects of our archaeological journey that make what we do relevant to people outside of our safe discipline. The human factor of our work takes away the sting of authority and scientific objectivity, which for some is the only direction post-contact archaeology should consider a part of its future (Franklin & McKee 2004, Agbe-Davies 2010, Franklin & Paynter 2010, Little & Zimmerman 2010, Mullins 2008, Bell 2008, Brandon 2008, Saitta 2007, Young 2004, Leone 2005, Palus et al. 2006, Little & Shackel 2007, Shackel 2010).

So, back to the "R" word. For a brief moment in early 2008 the United States was forced to think about, or at least begin a discussion centered on, Race, when the then Democratic presidential nominee, Senator Barack Obama, gave a reactive speech about the elusive topic. As we have witnessed throughout the twentieth and twenty-first centuries, racialization is a complicated and fluid process, and in that brief moment, we as a society needed to look critically at how race and racialization happen everyday and their effects on our society as a whole. As a beneficiary of the Civil Rights and Women's movements, I appreciate the struggles of my grandparents' and parents' generations; however, my generation often wonders what has happened since? This is why that moment of discussing Race in a national forum was so significant to scholars like myself, because it felt liberating, yet challenged many of us to find strategies for articulating our experiences that in the past had seemed too personal to bring to the forefront. This process became part of the motivation to write a book like *Black Feminist Archaeology*.

Thinking critically about Race has always been a part of my lived experience. I started my Ph.D. work at the University of Texas Austin in 1998, on the heels of the infamous "Hopwood decision." This case was brought by four individual plaintiffs (not a class of plaintiffs) who were denied admission to the University of Texas Law School in 1992, claiming that the Law School's admission process in 1992 violated the Fourteenth Amendment by giving race-based preferences exclusively to Blacks and Mexican Americans (Hopwood v. State of Texas, 861 F. Supp. 551 - Dist. Court WD Texas 1994). I found myself in the midst of an ever-increasing debate in the U. S. that questions the validity of Affirmative Action and race-based initiatives, the importance of Race as a determining factor of discriminatory practice, and a transition from overt racism to a new and veiled culturally based racism. Institutional and structural racism are more than abstract intellectual tirades; the lived reality can be seen in the poverty rates of children of African descent (as of 2009, 35.4 percent), the waning faith in "urban" public schools, and the growing numbers of African and Latino descended males in the prison industrial complex—all examples of the reality (National Poverty Center 2010, Davis 2003). Our political sensitivities have subliminally affected not only conservative speech, but realistic national dialogues. We cannot use the word apartheid (much more fitting) when referring to the Jim Crow era South as bell hooks does. We never say the word genocide when referring to the crack/drug epidemic that has plagued the inner cities of the United States for more than thirty years. We cannot use the word injustice to describe the institutional barriers placed before many of our nation's non-white populations. All these factors are directly tied to race and racism, class and classism, and sex and sexism. The problems we continue to face as a nation are often studied and analyzed within specific disciplines, but usually not brought to make structural or institutional changes on the ground. I believe there are ways to continue to expand these dialogues, make them seem more relevant to everyday people and allow for multiple generations and populations to have an impact on social transformation. I want to promote the idea that a field such as archaeology, one that is unique in many ways, can spark an interest in people and open a larger and more impactful discussion of our complicated past and present.

The final aspect of the idea of Race that I want to address is finding a definition of what it is to be of African descent in the Americas. The very thought of understanding Race in the New World has plagued scholars for decades (even centuries). I realize Race is a complex thought that has at its foundation a social construction based on economic pursuits and colonialism; however, because I see this as a fact of history, I believe that there is also a means to socially deconstruct this metaphor we live with so comfortably (Berlin 2000, Morgan 2003). We can understand the development of Race from the roots to the branches to the leaves. Race may never disappear, it is too entrenched in the psyche of the United States (and the world); however, we can challenge it, reshape it, and use its history as a way to transform how our future generations may see themselves. This is what honesty and reality can do in the quest to leave the ideas and legacies of Race behind us as a global community.

Becoming an Archaeologist

I came late to the field of archaeology. I must admit, I was first seduced by the artifacts, that stuff that is archaeology in its "purest," apolitical form. The first time I dug into the soil and "discovered" an artifact, I felt as if in my hands I was holding a piece of historical gold. It was so much stronger than reading a document or hearing a lecture or watching a documentary—it was a *real* piece of history. I entered the field in the mid-1990s, a time when plantation archaeology was the center of attention in Americanist archaeology. There were conferences dedicated to the topic, documentaries being made, and plentiful funding resources interested in the work of archaeologists working on African American sites. However, in this haze of archaeological seduction, I did not know that there would be moments when my credentials would be questioned, my "objectivity" would be critiqued, and my passion would be perceived as anger or rage. I often look back at the good and the bad and wonder why I remained an archaeologist. Perhaps it was my own tenacity, maybe my need to prove something or somebody wrong, or my chance to find a way to understand myself through an approach to the past that was grounded in material—the objects people left behind (Bolles 2001). For whatever reason, I am still here and this work has taught me volumes about myself, my past and the possibilities of how to convey what I have learned to future generations. It is also what has moved me mentally and physically from the environs of the Northeast Bronx to the academic halls of Western New England.

As a person of African descent I wanted to understand the history of my presence in this hemisphere. As are most people of African descent in the United States, I am a conglomerate of Africa, the Caribbean, Indigenous America, and European immigrants. I began with a passion for history, but often faced frustration and disappointment with the books I read and the classes I took in high school and college. My parents, especially my mother, pushed me to explore deeper, to use words to find my own truth from the fabricated tidbits and sorted facts of history in the United States. I did (superficially) learn about the Trail of Tears, but never heard mention of my people, the Eastern Band Cherokee, the ones who stayed in North Carolina. I heard about slavery and the scores of captive Africans, but was never given the language to understand the lasting legacy of enslavement in the colonial world, and never learned about Race, racism or my own invisibility in a concrete and realistic way during my educational experience. History never provided these details, and so I kept searching and wondering and longing.

After high school I wanted more than anything to get out of New York City. I wanted to go to a Historically Black College (HBCU) and decided on Virginia State University in Petersburg, Virginia. It was far from home, but close enough to get back if I needed an urban fix. Most of the student population was from the New York, New Jersey, and Connecticut tri-state area, which made the culture quite familiar, and served as a reaffirmation of my identity as an urban Black woman who made it "out" of the neighborhood. However, comfortable New Yorker or not, I was in the South (the Upper South) and things were very different. Within my first two years I learned about the politics of skin color, the social and political implications of how I wore my hair, my class position, and the ability to recognize a form of "in-your-face" racism that I was not accustomed to. I also learned that the North was not as Race neutral as I had grown up believing. Finally, the racism that I thought was a thing of my grandmother's generation, was not—it was alive and well and in many ways internalized by people of African descent in the North *and* South in ways that I was completely ignorant of.

I was a History and Education major and wanted to learn all I could about Africa. I wanted to understand the politics, the colonial legacy, the migrations, the second-wave diaspora, and the complexity of the continent. As an undergraduate, deep in the quest for an enriched vision of the continent, I became interested in slavery. I wanted to understand the system in all forms and all places. As my junior year ended I was torn, would it be graduate school or the Peace Corps. I chose graduate school and received a full scholarship to the Department of History at the College of William & Mary in Williamsburg, Virginia. Along with admission, I was offered a summer teaching assistantship at an archaeological field school at a plantation site in Williamsburg, working with then Berkeley graduate student Maria Franklin. I was nervous and afraid because I had not a moment of archaeology experience, but like a true New Yorker, I did not let that stop me. I let the prospect of graduate school settle in, packed some bags and a trunk, boarded a train to Williamsburg in 1994 and began a path that I continue to travel today.

My first experiences as an archaeologist were rosy and bright. I was surrounded by people with like minds. They were actively engaged in the pursuit of finding new and exciting ways of seeing the African American past. Our ideas were in constant conversation, and I was surrounded by people of color, progressive allies, and specialists that wanted to listen to our traditions and memories of the details of life and apply them to how they analyzed ceramics, faunal (animal) and plant remains. We had bone chewing parties, experiments with preparing one pot meals, and collaborative programs with the (former) Department of African American Interpretation and Presentations. This was the Colonial Williamsburg Foundation (CWF); I was a graduate intern at the Department of Archaeological Research, under the direction of Marley Brown, III. It was here that I began to learn about the foundations of historical archaeology. I was taught about ceramic analysis and museum display by William Pitman; studied a little bit about faunal analysis with Joanne Bowen; was exposed to phytolith (plant) analysis with Steve Mwrosowski; and introduced to landscape and garden archaeology with Mary Catherine Garden. The most impactful, however, was my participation in the public side of archaeological practice.

I was at Colonial Williamsburg at a historic and magical moment in post-contact archaeology. On any given day I was in the field with incredible archaeologists of African descent such as site director Maria Franklin, Anna Agbe-Davies, Ywone Edwards-Ingram, Jackie Denmon, and Cheryl LaRoche. I was spoiled and had no idea of the harsh world that awaited me once I left the confines of historic Williamsburg. What did happen in that incredible summer was that I was nurtured and allowed to grow intellectually, the next stage in my academic confidence building. I learned that I could be an archae-ologist that appreciated anthropological theory, history, the public, the past, and the African Diaspora simultaneously. I learned quickly that I needed to lean on that newly acquired academic confidence once out in the unmelodious world of *real* archaeology.

My journey would take me to many places, traveling from the rural Upper South to some cities in the Northeast. However, it was a 1,120 acre tract of land called the Hermitage Plantation in Hermitage, Tennessee, that would impact my life more than any other experience, teach me the realities of this field, and help me to understand how racism is real is in the United States and how per-ceptions of the past are different in different communities across the nation. I ask you to go with me on my journey as I remember what has happened in the past, look at what is happening around me now, and think about the future and all its possibilities.

Toward a Black Feminist Archaeology

A Black Feminist Archaeology is not a formula. It is a methodology that combines aspects of anthropological theory, ethnohistory, the narrative tradition, oral history, material culture studies, Black and African-descendant feminisms, and critical race and African Diaspora theories. It allows for a larger dialogue of how these theoretical approaches can be combined and used as lenses through which to understand the intersectionality of race, gender and class in the past.

The study of gender encompasses a wide variety of disciplines, topics, timelines and methodological approaches. Archaeologists have been addressing the questions of gender for generations. This has helped the field in moving ahead in the analysis of gender and gender systems from the pre-contact period, contact period and post-contact. These studies have forced practitioners to view the past through a gendered lens and include a methodology that seeks to understand the everyday lives of people and places often neglected by mainstream, gender neutral analyses. When addressing the lives of African descendant people, a gendered approach can mean capturing often neglected details and ignored elements of women, men and children of the past (King 1998, Wilkie 2003, Franklin 2001, Galle & Young 2004, Beaudry & Mrozowski 1989, Spencer-Wood 1991, Gero & Conkey 1991).

This book also provides a method for practitioners of archaeology to hear the voices of women of African descent throughout the diaspora (Guy-Sheftall 1995, hooks 2000, Davis 1981, Lorde 1982, Combahee River Collective 1982, Moraga & Anzaldua 1983, Carby 1987, Crenshaw 1989, Wallace [1979]1990, Collins 2000). The dialogue between women at all corners of the *New World* (including the French, Spanish and English speaking Caribbean, Brazil, Central and South America) has already begun. For the first time these voices are actively talking to each other and making their presence known. For example, the current wave of women of African descent who are writing about themselves in anthropology is increasing (McClaurin 2001, Ulysse 2008, Harrison 2008). For example, recognizing the historical denial of Afro-Latina and Latino communities (Dzidzienyo & Oboler 2005, Caldwell 2006, Candelario 2007), the erasure of women in self-liberated (also known as Maroon) communities in the Caribbean (Agorsah 1994, Deagan & MacMahon 1995, Weik 1997), the scarcity of scholarship on the cultural importance of women in places like Brazil, Cuba and Haiti (in the sense of religious practice, language, and cultural continuity), and finally a lack of attention paid to the hidden labor provided by women of African descent in the United States.

Black Feminist Archaeology is structured in four parts. The first part maps out what a Black Feminist archaeological methodology looks like. It provides a more detailed chronicle of my journey to archaeology and the ways the foundational structure of Black intellectual thought combined with Black feminism positively informs new and innovative approaches to understanding the lives and histories of women of African descent in the United States. The second part is a basic revision of my work at the Hermitage Museum, the plantation home of Andrew Jackson in Hermitage, Tennessee. I revisit my original research and apply a clearer and theoretically tighter analysis of women, family and domestic landscapes of a quarter neighborhood on the plantation. The third part of the book is a reanalysis of the Lucy Foster's homesite in Andover, Massachusetts. This homesite was excavated in 1942 by Ripley and Adelaide Bullen. It was among the first archaeological sites of an African American excavated in the United States. It for me is one of the foundations of African American archaeology; however, it has not factored into the historical memory of post-contact Americanist archaeology. The last part of the book is about my current and future research at the W. E. B. Du Bois Boyhood Homesite in Great Barrington, Massachusetts. My approach to this site is my addition to the ongoing work of Robert Paynter, who has been involved with the site since 1982. I use a Black Feminist framework to look at the previous archaeology and the material culture to bring gender, race and class together to begin to understand the neglected histories of African descendant women in Western Massachusetts. I am looking at the unique labor arrangement of second-home and hotel work and the historical invisibility of the women of the Burghardt family (Du Bois's maternal family).

This book has been in the making for many years, I would even say for many generations. The completion of this book is the culmination of one of my most cherished dreams, to begin to tell a story that is not just about archaeology or artifacts, but about people and places, women and men, leisure and labor, with details that can be relevant to contemporary struggles for social justice and liberation. In the words of my late grandmother H. Lawrencie Jones, life and struggle were not something that women of African descent (not a term she would be comfortable with) thought about or calculated, "It was just something we did as Black women." I hope that in some small way this book will continue in that tradition, one word at a time.

CHAPTER I

Constructing a Black Feminist Framework

I arrived at the Hermitage plantation during the second half of the sum-mer of 1996 as a five-week archaeological intern. I was excited to do archaeology on a real plantation site. I was nervous because this was my first time away from the safe and protected world of the Colonial Williamsburg Foundation. I had been there nearly two weeks and loved almost every aspect of the internship. However, there was something a little off that I could not yet explain. I was immersed in the full field experience; I was digging, eating, socializing, and living with the field crew. I was learning from archaeologists like Larry McKee (the director of the program) and Brian Thomas (the assistant director) and Jillian Galle (the field supervisor) and absorbing as much as I could. I had a lot to learn and was doing my best to make sure that I did not mess anything up. I loved to be in the dirt, in an excavation unit, finding artifacts and thinking about the people that were connected to all this material I was uncovering. All the archaeology was amazing, but some-times the down times were difficult. I was on a real plantation, and for me the energy was intense. There were times when I would think about the people who labored at the site, who lived, loved and died there as captives. It was really overwhelming at moments; I felt things that were hard to explain to my colleagues. I did not really understand how to process these feelings. There were general conversations about the field of archaeology and the specifics of what we were doing for the summer. Then there were the discussions of the African American past. This is when it would get uncomfortable for me. I had a four-year undergraduate degree in History Education from a Historically Black University where I had specialized in contemporary African history and culture. I had grown up with an educator mother invested in my knowing the African and African American past, had grown up in a vibrant African Traditionalist community, and I had a solid familiarity with most of the canons in the Black intellectual tradition. I began to even take those conversations personally; I never understood why everyone did not have this level of historical background in their preparation for digging at this site. Now, as a "fully-grown" archaeologist and academic, I do not blame the archaeologists that I met that summer, but I was taken off guard. Initially, I was angered. I wanted these archaeologists to be aware of the historical and contemporary issues facing people of African descent, and I wanted everyone to understand who the people were beyond a surface understanding of their lives and culture. I wanted them to see it my way, to prove to me that they were really about this thing we were calling African American archaeology. So, I was offended that the time had not been taken to understand not just slavery, but the struggles for recognition, acknowledgment and freedom. I thought about the complex arguments of W. E. B. Du Bois, Marcus Garvey, and Angela Davis, and I did not see this reflected anywhere in our conversations. For many reasons, I was not sure if this was the field for me. I was not confident that I could accept the lack of knowledge about my people within the discipline. That summer was long, hot and trying, but it was a summer that shaped the archaeologist I am today.

Introduction

Growing up Black and female in the United States is an exercise in skill, fortitude and perseverance. Early in my childhood I developed an awareness of an inability to express my frustration about racism, sexism, and just growing up female. This precarious combination of factors made for a complex web of emotion, anger and disconnect in how I would grow up and position myself in the larger world. As an adult, I became increasingly disillusioned by the arrogance of scholars from all types of disciplines giving "voice" to the silenced, forgotten souls of women of African descent. Frankly, as a woman of African descent, I never felt silenced in my life. Invisible, yes, but not silenced. There were many moments when I was screaming at the top of my lungs, only to look around and realize that no one was listening. As African Diasporic people, we understand that not every person's voice or story holds equal value in the past or present.

This country has never paid close attention to my existence. Women of African descent, here from the start of the colonial experience (Morton 1991), have remained marginal in comparison to men of African descent, Euroamerican women, and Euroamerican property owning men. This marginal existence can become quite bothersome and is why I profess that I have never been "silent," just busy, working, cleaning, nursing, raising, teaching, nurturing and existing for generations. The voices have not been silent, just in constant communication with other marginalized and subjugated women. We rarely have the time to contemplate how our stories will be remembered to a broader audience, part of the reason I argue we are often written about. The writing of our stories traditionally falls into the hands of scholars outside of the larger descendant community. From an early age, I was disillusioned by the way my sisters are often remembered, portrayed or characterized by historians, cultural critics, and popular media (duCille 1994, Morton 1991, Wallace 1990). However, as I grew older and decided that I wanted to engage in the work of historical archaeology, I noticed that overall in the academy our status as subject was rising, as chronicled by Ann duCille:

> Within and around the modern academy, racial and gender alterity has become a hot commodity that has claimed black women as its principle signifier. I am alternatively pleased, puzzled, and perturbed—bewitched, bothered, and bewildered—by this, by this alterity that is perpetually thrust upon African American women, by the production of black women as infinitely deconstructable

"othered" matter. Why are black women always already Other? I wonder. To myself, of course, I am not Other; to me it is the white women and men so intent on theorizing my difference who are the Other....The attention is not altogether unpleasant, especially after generations of neglect, but I am hardly alone in suspecting that the overwhelming interest in black women may have at least as much to do with the pluralism and perhaps the primitivism of this particular postmodern moment as with the stunning quality of black women's accomplishments and the breadth of their contributions to American civilization. (1994: 591–592)

For me, the works of African descendant women describing our own experiences become the most reliable source for developing a coherent theoretical dialogue about women in captivity and beyond. Black Feminist Archaeology, therefore, demonstrates through an analysis of the material past a method to positively enhance the texture and depth of how we understand the experiences of captive African peoples and further creates an archaeology that can be directly linked to the larger quest for social and political justice in the United States and beyond. Archaeology is neither race nor gender neutral, or absent of its share of racist, sexist, and social misunderstandings that are part of the larger history of the social sciences (Patten 1997, LaRoche & Blakey 1999, McDavid 1997). In addition, archaeology has demonstrated a traditionally slow paced reaction to change. Beneath all of this, however, is the reality of how we as experts do not want to be wrong about the work we do and how we come at our often personal methodological approaches to historic sites. Through a relatively new methodological approach like Black Feminist Archaeology, I argue, archaeologists can collaborate and create inclusive dialogues equipped with engaged research agendas to produce incredibly activist oriented outcomes that appeal to a multitude of audiences.

"Womanist Is to Feminist as Purple Is to Lavender"

When I decided to pursue a career in archaeology I predicted that my work would provide solutions to my own internal frustrations and solve the world's core problems. This premonition was quite naive, I will admit, but this belief continues to motivate me to find a realistic way to connect scholarship and real life issues. In the process I still experience extreme internal warfare stemming from my training in mainstream history and education and concern about how the larger archaeological audience will perceive my alternative approaches to the study of material culture. This internal battle I am referring to first began in my claiming a Black Feminist identity. My early experience with feminism was mostly an association with mainstream Euroamerican "stereotypical" ideas about being a feminist. I felt strongly that mainstream feminism was tied closely to consensus and compromise, therefore opposite of the Womanist philosophy (see definition below) I had fully embraced by that point. I really believed that the central tenets of the mainstream feminist philosophy could never fully embrace my cultural heritage or my needs as a woman of African descent. It was just not a "Black thing" (Hudson-Weems 2004, Walker 1983, Collins 2000, McClaurin 2001, hooks 2000). I also believed that this feminism, when claimed by women of African descent, was removed from the real struggles of Black life and community; it was an intellectual exercise that only the privileged could embrace (Morgan 2000). As my dissertation project was shaping and forming, I was trying very hard to avoid any association with the evil that "feminism" brings, but soon realized that the work I was doing was about the lived experience of captive African women, the captive family, and the complexity of domestic spaces, all topics marginalized in most androcentric perspectives. For me to demonstrate my commitment to understanding the juxtaposition of race and gender in the making of the female captive African subject, I discovered that archaeology was the right tool for this narrative. However, there needed to be some minor updates to how the discipline approached this topic methodologically. Initially, I was under the illusion that with the addition of materiality to my narrative of captive African domestic life, I could keep a superficial feminist approach and provide a deeper understanding of Black cultural production. So, I slowly expanded my cursory knowledge of Black

Feminist theory and literature to make up what was missing in my attempts at addressing race and gender.

> Womanist. From womanish. (Opposite of 'girlish,' i. e., frivolous, irresponsible, not serious.) A black feminist or feminist of color. From the black folk expression of mothers to female children, 'You acting womanish,' i.e., like a woman. Usually referring to outrageous, audacious, courageous or *willful* behavior. Wanting to know more and in greater depth than is considered 'good' for one. Interested in grown-up doings. Acting grown up. Being grown up. Interchangeable with another black expression: 'You trying o be grown.' Responsible. In charge. *Serious.* (Walker 1983: *xi*)

> *Also:* A woman who loves other women, sexually and/or nonsexually. Appreciates and prefers women's culture, women's emotional flexibility (values tears as natural counter-balance of laughter), and women's strength. Sometimes loves individual men, sexually and/or nonsexually. Committed to survival and wholeness of entire people, male *and* female. Not a separatist, except periodically, for health. (Walker 1983: *xi*)

Until the writing process, I maintained my identity as a Womanist [a term coined by Alice Walker that first appeared in Alice Walker's *Searching for Our Mother's Garden: A Womanist prose* (Walker 1983)]. I was not convinced that claiming a Black Feminist identity or doing "Black Feminist work" was right for me, even though it might have helped with the work I was doing (also see Franklin 2001, Wallace 2004, McClaurin 2001, Collins 2000, Morgan 2000). Simultaneously, I was feeling some pressure from my dissertation advisor, Maria Franklin, to seriously consider what Black Feminist theory really was. She urged me to look past my personal biases and look further into Black Feminist thought and theory. As I began this new relationship I searched for a connection to the mainstream feminism that I could not relate to. I needed answers to fill those gaps in my work where I felt that my methodological approach was disjointed, so I began to think through the process of how Black Feminist thought and theory could enhance what I was trying to do with archaeology.

I delved deeper into some classic Black Feminist texts and kept a critical eyebrow raised. However, I saw that Black Feminist theory provided a clearer way of seeing things, altered my initial conceptualizations of the historical narrative, the meaning behind artifacts, and the thinking through of a methodology that could be whole *and* healing. Around this juncture I discovered the words of the Combahee River Collective, a group of radical Black Feminists that gathered regularly from 1973 to 1980. They are best known for the Combahee River Collective Statement that chronicled the history of contemporary Black Feminism and the development of a broader understanding of an inclusive Black Feminist identity. This is one of the first statements that struck me:

> A political contribution which we feel we have already made is the expansion of the feminist principle that the personal is political. In our consciousness-raising sessions, for example, we have in many ways gone beyond white women's revelations because we are dealing with the implications of race and class as well as sex. Even our Black women's style of talking/testifying in Black language about what we have experienced has a resonance that is both cultural and political. We have spent a great deal of energy delving into the cultural and experimental nature of our oppression out of necessity because none of these matters has ever been looked at before. No one before has ever examined the multilayered texture of Black women's lives. (Combahee River Collective 1982)

Part of my own identity formation was connecting the personal with the political; it was how I wanted to structure my methodology. I understood the impact of not only focusing on gender in my work, but how certain "innocent" assumptions often play an active role in contemporary forms of racialized and gendered stereotypes. For example, one of my fears was that my work could mistakingly be perceived as reproducing old imageries of a broken and dysfunctional Black family forced by captivity into a non-patriarchal, therefore "pathological" (women-centered) family structure. This would then lead to yet another analysis of the exploded sense of the "strong Black woman" as a way of understanding Black culture and the Black family (Wallace 1999). This imagery is a part of the complexity of writing about race and gender in the past. There are very real contemporary implications to how archaeologists shape their larger interpretations.

The role of women of African descent in the historical memory of the United States is fraught with misconceptions, misgivings and stereotypes. Whether negative or positive, they are fully entangled in the way women of African descent are perceived generally. Motherhood and mainstream ideals of the feminine is a realm that I briefly explored in my dissertation about racialized femininity and representation of women of African descent through time. A central theme in the experiences of captive African women was sexual exploitation and abuse. These themes were often left out of the literature of the time (for example see Harriet Jacobs narrative, Yellen 1987) because the women writing their stories needed to appear as sexually pure as possible to appeal to abolitionists and Euroamerican women caught in a very real Victorian mindset (Patten 1999). So, I had to be sensitive about how I approached the topic of women, family and female/male relationships. An example would be the emphasis of, and (often exaggerated) importance of, Black women as culture bearers. On the ground level, this categorization is so normalized in our historical imagination that it is almost impossible to separate the myth of the overbearing Black woman from the image of a collective, at times semi-egalitarian captive and then freed community. With an attempt to highlight the absence of women of African descent in the larger understanding of the colonial and antebellum past, a gendered analysis has to be extra careful with the words and images that are created by the work. I do not want to attempt to create an image of the Black domestic sphere as without fault or simply in opposition to the evil norm of Euroamerican patriarchal culture. Things were not perfect, and the ability to create an egalitarian social system in a captive context is probably a theoretical stretch in many ways. I recognized that there was a form of internalized patriarchy that was a real aspect of life within a captive community. The inability of captive African men to actively pursue their patriarchal destiny was controlled in very dehumanizing ways by plantation owners and overseers. Captive men were thrust into a society ruled by a patriarchal design; however, they could not actively participate as property themselves. There was a severe disadvantage in their inability to protect the women and children in their "families." With this in mind, my theoretical approach had to acknowledge that captive men were directly affected by this contradiction of core social systems of colonial and antebellum America and the reality of their lived situation.

Therefore, to shape an interpretation of the captive African domestic sphere, there had to be a larger understanding of how women of African descent were viewed in the past and present. Archaeological material is important to a discussion of issues of resistance, family formation, and daily life; however at the same time, archaeology has to contend with the reality of racialized and gendered stereotypes of captive women and men. I did not want to "mistakenly" recreate an image of emasculating captive women and weak, unproductive captive men, nor glorify the captive domestic sphere as the template for all understanding of Black domestic cultural production. This one issue had, for me, a lot more baggage attached to my interpretation than just seeing the value of captive women shaping their family's domestic spaces, an example of the sensitivity of a Black Feminist Archaeological approach.

Identity Formation and Black Women's Fiction

In my writing I began to actively engage with these issues of contemporary African America without placing modern notions of social or racialized political elements onto my interpretations of the past. I searched for sources that addressed my needs and questions of the African American past from a gendered perspective. I knew the written sources would be scarce, but never imagined that they would border on nonexistent. I searched for material that could address my questions, compliment my developing interpretative frameworks, and potentially confront historical inconsistencies I was sure to encounter. Black women's fiction had always spoken to me at different points in my life and career. I used these texts when I was depressed, lonely, sad or homesick. I savored the words of wise warrior women in ways that helped me to fight the good fight and continue to see my value, knowing that one day I too wanted to touch the world with the narrative of my own struggles and experiences. However, as a trained historian that was now an anthropological archaeologist, I felt extremely uneasy about using literature or my own history in a way that was academically acceptable.

The connection between contemporary Black women writers and slavery is found in the ways that gender articulates with race in the contemporary work of these women (Patton 1999: xiv). In fact, the very foundation of Black feminist thought is linked to the de-gendering process experienced by Black women during slavery throughout the African Diaspora. Venetria Patton explains this process as the "institution's attempt to de-gender female slaves and their resistance to such tactics generated alternative gender constructs. Due to the socially constructed nature of maternity, slave mothers and their descendants formulated different maternal ideals than white mothers" (1999). Therefore, the Black literary tradition is often a response to the conventional representation of women of African descent in their own words. Patton addresses this issue in her discussion of Black women's fiction: "Just as female slaves developed a different conception of gender identity, later Black women writers created a different means of approaching the subject. Often Black women writers did not find the methods of white women writers fully satisfying because they were working with different ideas about gender as well as different receptions of their gender" (2000: xiv).

I consulted the works of writers such as Harriet Jacobs, born into captivity in Edenton, North Carolina, escaped from James Norcom in 1835, after over a decade of sexual abuse. She took on a consensual affair with a free white lawyer, Samuel Sawyer, and had two children who were the property of Norcom by law. After her escape, she hid in a few places and then concealed herself in the crawlspace of her grandmother's attic for seven years. This act allowed her to be "free" from Norcom, keep a watchful eye on her children, still in captivity, and in many ways regain her own sense of humanity (Yellen

1987). Her story was thought provoking and spoke directly to the often misunderstood relationship between mothers in captivity and their children. I also looked to Mary Prince, a captive woman born in Brackish Pond, Bermuda, in 1788. Her story was one of great pain, hardship and a quest for freedom that is usually never ascribed to captive African women (Prince 1998). Her worth was entangled in her labor and once her body could no longer perform expected tasks, her life was seen as valueless. At the core of her story was a quest to get her freedom and live her life with her freed husband, which seemed nearly impossible under the circumstances of her captivity.

An additional aspect of the Black literary tradition is the contemporary novel and its direct connection to identity formation through the narrative of captivity. Toni Morrison's *Beloved* is one of the best examples of how captivity affected African women, men, children and the captive and freed families of the period. The touching and tragic story of Sethe is essentially about a mother's love, a father's inability to protect his family from within the system of slavery, death, and the fragility of freedom (Morrison 1987). The novel was saturated with imagery and texture that could only be used in fiction; however, the way Morrison described the captive and free landscape was telling of how people of African descent remember their past. Within her words lived pain, memory, love and disappointment, but for me the most important factor was the alternate imagery of family. Morrison understood the complexity of the captive family in ways that cannot be proven by the document or historic account; instead there is a spiritual and emotional truth that touches the reader in a meaningful and lasting way. The last of my top four literary sources was Gayl Jones's equally painful saga *Corregidora*. Jones chronicles the lives of four generations of women who are the descendants of a brutal Brazilian enslaver, whose sexual exploitations of these women became the story of their identity and truth (Jones 1987). It was through their words that the truth would never die, even if all the evidence was burned or forgotten; it was through the Corregidora maternal line that the brutal nature of captivity would live on as a testament to a tragic past. However, the main character, Ursa, has a tragic accident and cannot have children. This is initially seen as the end of the line, the end of the story; however, through singing the blues she discovers a way (other than being a mother) to tell the story of her ancestors, continuing the tradition of storytelling as a form of healing.

These works became the thread that tied together the incredible stories of women that were not recreating a mythical past, but tied my approach to interpretation with a real sense of how African descendant identity formation has changed through time. These works were also a testament of the various methods that African descendant women choose to tell their own stories. In the genre titled the "neo-slave narrative" is the fluid way in which stories of captivity are directly tied to contemporary African Diasporan identity formation across the Western Hemisphere (Rushdy 1999). In my childhood, I was aware of issues of slavery, oppression and how books were a part of how we learned about history, and I have distinct memories at the age of six, sitting with my mother on our huge brown velvety couch watching *Roots*, the mini series. Stories of survival were not seen as strictly heroic; they were imbedded with lessons and memories that would always be outside of the realm of formal education. In high school and then college, I delved head first into classic historical texts on slavery and the scholarship of African American history and culture (for example, Phillips 1918, Stampp 1989, Herskovitz 1969, Frazier 1939, Elkins 1976, Gutman 1977, Genovese 1976, Blassingame 1979, Stuckey 1988, Raboteau 1980).

To understand the unique forms of oppression experienced by captive women, these texts were essential to my creating that textured understanding of racist and sexist forms of oppression. In addition to the shifting of narrative authority, I knew there was an obligation to place my work into a larger genealogy of Black Feminist theoreticians. As Barbara Christian so eloquently describes:

'If black women don't say who they are, other people will and say it badly for them,' I say, as I remember Audre Lordes' poem about the deadly consequences of silence. 'Silence is hardly golden,' I continue. 'If other black women don't answer back, who will?

When we speak and answer back we validate our experiences. We say we *are* important, if only to ourselves.' (1985:xi)

In my forming of this Black Feminist guided archaeology, I asked myself a very basic question: why is it such an arduous task to talk honestly and critically about Black women? Could it only be the domain of Black women to interpret a past that includes both gender *and* race? Is it that difficult to understand our invisibility on the historical landscape? The inability to talk about us reinforces the myth of our virtual (and unrealistic) invisibility as perhaps a partial reason that we remain such a perplexing topic. There is a fear that talking about Black women is plagued by misunderstanding, stereotypes, and myth building, so it seems easier for us to approach from a surface analysis.

However, a Black Feminist Archaeology can open up the dialogue a bit further to include different interpretations of the racially gendered past. Especially because the even deeper essential question of who can talk about us is to understand that it is not easy even for us "Sister Scholars" to maintain a viable dialogue. We are human and struggle with an inability to maintain lasting internal dialogues with each other. As I have come to learn in writing this book, when the words come together they can be liberating and painful simultaneously. This is hard work, filled with self-doubt and peppered with all of our personal and professional inconsistencies, family and community obligations, and the work of life that often equates to interesting forms of exhaustion. Whether we see ourselves as Black feminists, Womanists, Africana Womanists, Afrodescendant feminists, Afro-Latina feminists, African feminists, Third Wave Feminists or African descendant women inside or outside the academy, our identities are a constant source of self analysis, debate and dialogue.

So, it remains the Black literary tradition, born from the memories of fugitive women and men who wanted to bear witness and share the horrific historical experience of life under captivity, that still in many ways unites all of these conflicted, yet related identities. While time withered away the physical bondage, the psychological effects of the captivity lingered. It was through literature that the painful connection with the past was articulated for contemporary audiences. In a similar fashion to popular Victorian women's literature, these writers enabled future generations to explore age-old questions in ways that were both creative and therapeutic. Toni Morrison's idea of "re-memory" as a defining moment of Black cultural reproduction is a perfect example (Morrison 1993). For Black women, re-memory is not based on lived experience, but on a fluid relationship with captivity and how the conscious silencing of Black women continues to shape their lives across time.

Although these works of fiction did help me through some rough times, I was able to incorporate them into the development of my theoretical approach to my archaeological work. It was the ability to see outside of the archaeological toolbox that allowed me to value these texts in a way that filled very obvious gaps in my larger discussion of captive life at a place like the Hermitage or the W. E. B. Du Bois Boyhood Homesite. These works have also allowed extremely interesting conversations with friends and colleagues outside of archaeology, and especially discussions with members of my own and other communities of color. When you begin a talk with a quote from Toni Morrison or Gayl Jones, the conversation is not centered on research or interpretive outcomes; it becomes a dialogue about a painful, relatable and powerful past.

Household and Gender in Archaeology

> I have long been puzzled by two questions about archaeology which derive from my feminist commitments. First, why is there no counterpart in archaeology to the vibrant traditions of research on women and gender now well established in most other social scientific fields? And, second, what are the prospects, at this juncture, for the development of an archaeology of gender? (Wylie 1991: 31)

I read this passage many years ago as a graduate student struggling not only with the lack of focus on gender in post-contact archaeology, but my own commitment to a feminism of any sort. So, sitting down to write about gender in archaeology and the push for a feminist archaeology I turned to a classic, *Engendering Archaeology* by Joan Gero and Margaret Conkey. I also turned to another classic, Alison Wylie's article, "Gender Theory and the Archaeological Record: Why Is There No Archaeology of Gender?" I could see that the arguments of why it was important to ask the questions, the overall implications of not including gender, and the need to push to initiate parallels with other disciplines hit very close to home.

I was still carrying the baggage of my mistrust of the equal rights movement, second-wave feminism and exclusionary practice based on class, race and sexuality. I admit, this is a very narrow understanding of the movement—the struggles of middle-class white women and, most importantly, feminist studies within the academy were a bit unfounded. However, these first articles I read on gender in archaeological practice were a part of the shaping of the ever-illusive development of my own theoretical approach. I read about gendered perspectives on pre-contact sites in the Northeast and Mesoamerican sites in the larger Americas; however, much of the discussion did not relate to the post-contact North American sites I was interested in (Gero & Conkey 1991, Brumfeld 1991, Spector 1993, Wright 1996, Claassen 1997, Hays-Gilpin & Whitley 1998). So, I delved further and explored gender and feminism in post-contact archaeology. I was surprised at how much I related to the work of key women in the field addressing very exciting and troublesome questions of the material and documentary record (Rotman 2009, Wall 1994, Spencer-Wood 1991, Beaudry 1989, Wall 1994, Little 1994a). These approaches critically questioned non-feminist analyses of issues like "gender power dynamics," the conflation of gender with biological sex, and the uncritical acceptance of "dominant patriarchal gender ideology" (Spencer-Wood 2006: 60).

The archaeology of gender thinks critically about a woman such as Lucy Foster, a freedwoman who lives in a house on the main road with a lifetime of experiences and stories. A gendered lens can reshape the discussion of who she was and the possible alternative ways to see her as a woman. As a freedwoman, she could have been an active part of the local economy, a dedicated member of the local church, a safe house for escapees traveling northward, or a woman who held an important place in the Andover community. This approach also allows for a different way to view the ancestral home lot of generations of a New England African American family named the Burghardts. We can begin to think about the way that women shaped the familial landscape and established a compelling story of persistence, perseverance, and strength. Archaeologically, I successfully argued that the "communal" nature of the captive household cannot maintain or withstand mainstream, rigid inter-pretations of a "gender division" of space. It seems superficial to assume a "women versus men" framework when interpreting the lives of captive African people. It flattens the layered components of Black cultural production, practiced throughout the African Diaspora, colonial, and postcolonial West Africa. Therefore, my experience with mainstream gender archaeology was positive, but left me wanting a more nuanced approach to the very specific needs of my archaeological work.

There continues to be an increasingly deeper analysis of African American and African Diasporic sites, especially those revolved around the exploration of households (for example, see Beaudry & Mrozowski 1989, Spencer-Wood 1991, Wilkie 2000, Fesler 2004, Franklin 1997a, Barile & Brandon 2004, Battle-Baptiste 2008). My first engagement with household archaeology was situated across Mesoamerica, Thailand, Southern Africa and Australia (Allison 1999, Wilk & Rathje 1982, Netting 1984, Blier 1995, Hamilton 1988, Brumfiel 1991, Kuper 1993, Glassie 1975). These sites helped as a foundation for my understanding of archaeological approaches to various household structures, especially along the lines of social and cultural performance that resonated with my own research. My work on the captive household highlighted the collective nature of a multiple family domestic social system that allowed for the cap-tive community on one plantation to create, structure and maintain a cohesive and nurturing domestic space. I then expanded how I defined family to include the fluidity of captive African kinship networks. My conclusion was the development of a theory where the domestic sphere as the location of a "complex household," which included the ways captive communities shaped and manipulated their immediate living situations. So, my perceptions of the captive family had to change over time. Initially, I was trying to define the household similar to the work of household archaeologists such as Wilk, Rathje, Allison, and Netting: however, there remained anomalies in the overall analysis that kept me from getting to the conclusions I knew were there (Davis 1981, Morton 1991, Patton 1999, Beaudry 1993, Spencer-Wood 1991, Yentsch 1994).

As I looked for a deeper reading of the captive African family in history and literature, I immediately uncovered a huge mess. I knew that I wanted to contextualize my work on the captive African family, the plantation and its surrounding landscapes. However, trying to get at the Black family was like slowly opening Pandora's box; it got ugly quickly. The constant emphasis on the recurring role of overbearing women of African descent was not what I expected. There was a repetitive quality to the arguments of these women as anti-patriarchal, hyper-emasculating, and the progenitors of the flawed Black matriarchal tradition. I was well aware that the Black family had been the subject of research, sociological inquiry and the topic of domestic ethnography for more than one hundred years (Du Bois 1890, Hurston 1995, Drake & Cayton 1993, Frazier 1939, Herskovits 1941, Moynihan 1964, Stack 1974, Genovese 1974, Gutman 1976, Blassingame 1978, Davis 1981, Malone 1992, Fox-Genovese 1988, Walsh 1997), but I had no idea how all of this negative "press" was going to help my research or my dissertation. As I reread Du Bois's *Philadelphia Negro* (1890) and turned the pages of E. Franklin Frazier's *The Negro Family in the United States* (1939), I quickly understood why it was necessary to go down this path to get to the conclusions and context-building content I so subconsciously craved. I was able to securely pinpoint how captivity and contemporary misconceptions of the Black family were directly related (see Gutman 1977). Frazier argued that it was the institution of slavery that provided the foundation for Black women to assume a "dominant" role in the family structure. Though there are merits to some aspects of Frazier's thesis, his model adopted a Eurocentric patriarchal family structure as the ideal. This was the path that in my opinion led to the U. S. Department of Labor commission's infamous *The Negro Family: The Case for National Action* less than thirty years later. Better known as the "Moynihan Report," this sociological study became the means to understand the reasons behind Black poverty, family disunity, widespread under-education, and under-employment. This was the background noise that I, as an archaeologist, needed to be cognizant of as I entered the world of interpreting the African American past in the United States and the larger diasporic world.

There is a starting point, where we can subconsciously carry perceptions of the African Diaspora that begin with a comfortable placement of Eurocentrism in our understanding everything from language, religion, and family structure to social and cultural mores and norms. However, imagine if as scholars we could think about the African past in the New World from a more intricate view of creolization and cultural exchange. For example, James Sweet (2003:229) suggests that instead of starting from a theory of creolization when analyzing African culture, "we should assume that specific African cultural forms and systems of thought survived intact. We should then assess these disparate cultural and ethnic streams and attempt to chart the *process* of creolization." This could offer very different perceptions of how captive communities envisioned their environment, their immediate communities, and their own cultural production. It would also influence the way that scholars of the African Diaspora shape their interpretive frameworks.

I have argued that the perceived dominant role of women of African descent was not based so much on control as it was on the maintenance of African American culture. Angela Davis (1981) asserts that it was the domestic sphere that became the space of identity and cultural formation. I believe that archaeology complicates simplistic notions of overbearing Black women and absent Black men. The reality of slavery must be considered when thinking about the construction and development of captive African social systems. Women and men were both working with a constant level of labor expectations. As captives, they were often assigned very different, however equally taxing, jobs and tasks. The reality of women actively shaping and maintaining the domestic sphere was an unrealistic, but expected remnant of white mainstream patriarchy. Captive men were working and actively shaping the larger plantation environment, from clearing fields, to constructing buildings, to learning crafts and trades, to hunting, etc. However, the other incredible thing that I have learned since my dissertation project, is how these seemingly disparate forms of labor all met back home in the quarters, and archaeologically, I have evidence that at central places there were gatherings of women, men, elders and children, all sharing in domestic and social production in ways that can be overlooked by the analysis of captive life through documents.

Ultimately, captive African families differed from those of both their African homelands and their Euroamerican captors. Simultaneously, there were also aspects of African cultural and family practices that were reinforced by the conditions of slavery—including fictive kin networks, premarital or bridal pregnancy, diffuse responsibility for parenting, and women-centered domestic production (Robertson 1996, White 1999). Yet, the typical view of captive family formation does not take into account its African roots or the dire consequences that slavery had on family structure. Rather, as Claire Robertson (1996:18) argues, it is the sexist and racist assumptions of the matrifocal/matriarchal arguments that underlie these stereotypical representations of Black family structure.

When we actively acknowledge where we stand when we enter the arena of archaeological interpretation, we will begin to create a space that initially may seem uncomfortable, but will allow us to use an inclusive and inquiring approach to the sites we are excavating. It is all very confusing, and I think that is the exciting part, an aspect that I feel a Black Feminist Archaeology is a part of.

An African Diaspora of Inclusion

The idea of the African Diaspora is both a fluid and malleable concept. It is not singularly a place or a theory, but can be considered a part of an identity, a connection with a homeland, or the recognition of a separation from an ancestral place. The African Diaspora is imbued with power, and I want this power to become part of a larger understanding of the strength of this diaspora in archaeological practice. In addition, the African Diaspora has a temporality and spaciality that is often overlooked in historical archaeology. This is where a global dialogue adds value to our work on a multitude of levels. It strengthens our larger understanding of the people whose material we find on a daily basis and allows for a real conversation, where we can actively learn from each other about how material enhances our understanding of such intense transformations on both sides of the Atlantic Ocean.

The term African Diaspora did not really form fully until the 1950s and 1960s and served scholarly debates as both a political term and an essentialist way of seeing things. There was an attempt "to emphasize unifying experiences of African people dispersed by the slave trade" (Patterson & Kelley 2000). "The making of a 'black Atlantic' culture and identity and pan-Africanism, was as much the product of 'the West' as it was of internal developments in Africa" (Gilroy 1993). Racial capitalism, imperialism, and colonialism—the process that created the current African Diaspora—shaped African culture(s) while transforming Western culture itself (Patterson & Kelley 2000:13).

Much of this was to also look at the role of people of African descent in the transformation and creation of new cultures, institutions, and ideas inside and outside of Africa. In 2000, Tiffany Patterson and Robin D. G. Kelley clearly state:

> The presumption that black people worldwide share a common culture was not, as we have already suggested, the result of poor scholarship. It responded to a political imperative—one that led to the formation of political and cultural movements premised on international solidarity. Thus, while acknowledging the

African cultural survivals in the New World, we must always keep in mind that diasporic identities are socially and historically constituted, reconstituted, and reproduced; and that any sense of a collective identity among black peoples in the New World, Europe, and Africa is contingent and constantly shifting. Neither the fact of blackness nor shared experiences under racism nor the historical process of their dispersal makes for community or even a common identity. (2000:19)

As a student of the African Diaspora, I also recognize that the African Diaspora can be both process and condition (Patterson & Kelley 2000). It cannot be learned or fixed in *any* permanent form, for it is lived, experienced, altered and denied simultaneously. To understand a small portion of the complexity of the African Diaspora, there must be an acknowledgement of the various experiences of people of African descent. The multiple waves of dispersal, voluntary and involuntary immigration, political migration and immigration, back and forth relocation, and varying forms of expatriation are just some of the ways that one can move through the diasporan maze. However, most important is the development of an African diasporic identity that can dictate and often define how you live in a particular place.

Much of the confusion I faced when attempting to grasp the complicated web of African Diasporan identity was that a major component was missing in much of the scholarship on the African Diaspora coming from the continental United States. There was a precarious displacement of Africa, colonial or post-colonial. Archaeologists, especially, were discussing influences, cultural continuums, traces of diasporic identities in the material; however, I never really saw the direct connections being made with work done in the Atlantic African region (for larger discussion see DeCorse 1999, Posnansky 1999, Ogundiran & Falola 2007). I want to reinsert Africa into the larger discussion of the African Diaspora as a way to enhance how our research flows, is appreciated and interpreted within and outside the field. I have always worked from a personal African worldview, even when I knew it may not be understood by all. This perspective informed my overall approach to interpretation. However, I have also been guilty of rarely engaging with my Africanist colleagues while I was professing to be seeing things through an African Diaspora perspective. This was another example of how casual conversations and old friendships (and attending my first African Studies Association meeting) allowed me to see my own shortcomings. It is a practice that I feel needs to move beyond intellectual speculation into action.

This conundrum of engagement is not rare in African Diaspora archaeology. As Paul Mullins warns,

> The archaeological details of everyday diasporan agency, however, risk becoming detached from the concrete structural impressions of global racism and Atlantic cultural connections that remain at the heart of almost all diasporan scholarship. Elevating the individual agent may have its own problematic political impacts if archaeologists reproduce a distinctly European sense of individualism, and if diasporan archaeologies fail to address globality, they risk losing significant sociopolitical power. ([Meskell 2002:285] Mullins 2008:109)

To profess an ability to interpret the material of the African American past from an African worldview is a dangerous statement. These words are heavy with responsibility. The task is not impossible, but something I assumed would be intuitive. It was not and will never be; it takes real work, real communication and research and thought to grasp and be able to apply this knowledge to the larger archaeological record (Delle 1998, Perry 1998, Perry & Paynter 1999).

There was a quick shift in historical archaeology from what was considered Plantation archaeology or African American archaeology to what is now called African Diaspora archaeology. This trend has always made me uneasy, because the terms and perceptions of African Diaspora theory are complex and easily misunderstood or exaggerated. Scholars of the African Diaspora are constantly debating, altering, shifting, and refining how to define their own theoretical frameworks. Just as there are Black Feminisms, the ideas and meanings of being of African descent are very local in their creation and their maintenance (Gordon 1998).

We need to take into account the fact that there is no one definition of an African Diaspora, no single unifying language, no monolithic or single culture. Instead it is many things simultaneously. It is a sense of belonging to something larger than the individual. The collective is fluid; there is no way to pinpoint exactly what this notion is because it is forever changing, growing or shrinking. Paul Mullins asserts, "There are complicated effects to forging a European sense of individuality that does not confront the relationship between race and agency or the power of racial consciousness among diasporan peoples" (2008:110).

For gender hierarchy, there is an interesting question about what was a Western influence versus a distinctly West and Central African notion of female and female relationships (Robertson 1996). Also, there are real marked differences in gender hierarchies on the content and throughout the African Diaspora. An often cited example is the difference between the role of women in African traditional systems and their role in African and African American Christian systems. Both women and men hold positions of power. In the Yoruba language there is no word for woman or man. In the spiritual realm, gender is a non-issue, for there is more emphasis on the power and the relations between God and human, human and nature (Vodou, Myalism, Obeah, and Yoruba) (Thompson 1984, Brown & Cooper 1990, Leone & Fry 1999, Wilkie 1995, Clark 2005, Fennell 2007).

Diaspora has always been about inclusion and exclusion simultaneously. To be within a system while always maintaining a marginalized presence is a part of a legacy brought on by colonialism and maintained by racism and classism. It is for these reasons that the African Diaspora can benefit from using forms of strategic essentialism (also characterized as Pan-Africanism). According to Gayatri Chakravorty Spivak, this strategy uses group identity as the basis for struggle, even if temporarily. Her strategies for whom she describes as the subaltern allows for people of African descent to move away from hegemonic notions of power, oppression and false political consciousness (Fanon 1952,

Gramsci 1971, Spivak 1995). A great deal of this scholarship came from a political need for change and self acknowledgement. This is the strength of a strategic essentialist project in the African Diaspora, a method to use the history of captivity and oppression in ways that lead directly to social justice for peoples of African descent.

Black Feminist Thought

> As a critical social theory, Black feminist thought aims to empower African-American women within the context of social injustice sustained by intersecting oppressions. Since Black women cannot be fully empowered unless intersecting oppressions themselves are eliminated, Black feminist thought supports broad principles of social justice that transcend U. S. Black women's particular needs. (Collins 2000: 22)

> Above all else, our politics initially sprang from the shared belief that Black women are inherently valuable, that our liberation is a necessity not as an aside, but as a basic need of human beings for autonomy. This may seem so obvious as to sound simplistic, but it is apparent that no other ostensibly progressive movement has ever considered our specific oppression as a priority or worked seriously for the ending of that oppression. Merely naming the pejorative stereotypes attributed to Black women (e.g. mammy, matriarch, Sapphire, whore, bulldagger), let alone cataloguing the cruel, often murderous, treatment we receive, indicates how little value has been placed upon our lives during four centuries of bondage in the Western hemisphere. We realize that the only people who care enough about us to work consistently for our liberation are us. Our politics evolve from a healthy love for ourselves, our sisters and our community which allows us to continue our struggle and work. (The Combahee River Collective 1982)

When one writes about Black Feminist Thought there are many things to consider. How strong you make your arguments, how carefully you choose your words, and most of all, how purposeful you are in telling a story filled with pain, personal politics and anger. Writing about the history of the feminist movement and the intimate relationship between racism and sexism was a difficult aspect of this book. However, as difficult as it may be, relaying the painful past is probably one of the most foundational aspects of my own personal intellectual identity formation. Understanding that I am first racialized as Black and then further marginalized as a woman in many ways forced me to choose between these two linked identities. These internal politics are at the core of the disjunction between African descendant women and Euroamerican women from as far back as the Woman's Suffrage Movement (Giddings 1984). Take into account how the myth of Sojourner Truth and her words during the 1851 Akron Women's Rights convention, where she held up her bare arm and spoke the words, "ar'n't I a woman," solidifies in many ways that women of African descent were ever present in the struggle for women's rights. However, based on solid and painstakingly thorough research by Nell Irvin Painter, the reality is that these words and brief speech may have been the inventive writing of one Frances Dana Gage (Painter 1996). The fact that we have always known these words, this incredible strength that has always defined Sojourner Truth, may in reality have been the creation of someone else's vision of how a woman of African descent brought a different perspective to the struggle and in symbolic ways proved that the movement included issues of gender *and* race (Painter 1996, Sánchez-Eppler 1998).

The inability to remove race and/or racism from the argument has never been an option for women of African descent. Paula Giddings, author of the first collection of narrative histories of African American women, *When and Where I Enter*, summarizes this reality:

> The means of oppression differed across race and sex lines, but the wellspring of that oppression was the same. Black women understood this dynamic. White women, by and large, did not. White feminists often acquiesced to racist ideology, undermining their own cause in doing so. For just as there is a relationship

between racism and sexism, there is also a connection between the advance of Blacks and that of women. The greatest gains made by women have come in the wake of strident Black demands for their rights. (1984:6)

A significant factor in the history of Black Feminist political thought is the common experiences of Black women's employment after World War II. "Black women worked primarily in two occupations—agriculture and domestic work. Their ghettoization in domestic work sparked an important contradiction. Domestic work fostered U. S. Black women's economic exploitation, yet it simultaneously created the conditions for distinctively Black and female forms of resistance" (Collins 2000). Although close relationships were forged by the intimacy of domestic work, Black women fully understood that they remained "economically exploited workers and thus would remain outsiders" (Collins 2000). These experiences not only formed a connection between Black women, but also allowed women of African descent to view different angles of the vision of oppression.

When Betty Friedan's *The Feminine Mystique* was published in 1963 it was credited as being one of the foundational texts for contemporary feminist thought. It marked a moment when Euroamerican suburban women were seeking meaningful jobs outside of the home and the ability to play their role in the world (Giddings 1984, hooks 1984). This thought process was completely alien to women of African descent. These women were working outside of the home, preforming heroic acts, marrying and having children. This was the time of the Civil Rights movement, the golden age of the Student Nonviolent Coordinating Committee, and "group centered" egalitarian organizing strategies to fight racial oppression in the United States (Giddings 1984:300). The interracial fight for Civil Rights was not just fraught with internal disputes, but also racial tensions between Euroamerican and African descent women. One of the main conflicts was the dissatisfaction of Euroamerican women who did not agree with the primacy of race over issues of gender discrimination. The tensions led to an increasingly contentious relationship between these groups of women that would ensure the marginal position of race and women of African descent in the larger mainstream feminist movement of the 1970s and 1980s. Patricia Hill Collins describes how this tension led to further omissions of Black women's voices in the mainstream feminist movement.

The reality of this period was that the dominant feminist discourse never took into account that the lived experiences of women were different across racial and class lines. There was an abundance of race and class biases in the writings of Euroamerican feminists. In the history of the United States, class struggles have always been linked to struggles to end racism (hooks 1984). The suffering of Euroamerican upper and middle-class women may have been plagued with particular struggles; however, women of African descent, Latina women, and lower class Euroamerican women were not fighting the same fights; the collectivity of womanhood was not universal. The issues that were central to these variant groups found no real home in the mainstream feminist movement.

So, the way that many young women of African descent were introduced to feminist theory was through the ideal of Womanism, that not only challenged mainstream ideas of feminism, but dismissed it as a movement that did not include us. We as young women of African descent had benefitted from our grandmothers', mothers' and aunts' struggles during the Civil Rights Movement, the Women's Liberation Movement, etc. So, we never really understood what it was like to be denied a job based on our gender or not having the ability to question what was fair pay. However, we did understand how it felt to be followed around a retail store or be ignored by the sales clerk because we were Black. Again, as in generations past, the feminist struggle was someone else's struggle, one from which we benefitted, however marginally. This is how I came to understand that internal struggle to claim a feminist identity.

After completing my Ph.D. in anthropology, I accepted a postdoctoral appointment at the Africana Studies and Research Center at Cornell University. I quickly realized how inexperienced as a Black Feminist I was. Cornell was a department with a unique history of political and social activism, but was in reality a very masculine place. The first year was filled with great exchanges, dialogues, and a constant interaction with the local community and the graduate students. All that transpired between those halls kept me thinking constantly. The experience allowed me to begin to see the direction I wanted to take my work. I could see the threads of public scholarship and Black Feminist thought coming together as I had never experienced it in archaeology, and I still had the goal to develop a methodology that could work to heal my own feelings of invisibility and suppression. During my transition from graduate student to not-quite junior faculty, I also began to combine the various research approaches to more fully form my academic identity, especially when faced with students of color that had the same skepticism I had before about Black Feminism. In a place where Black Feminist theory was not front and center, I was remarkably at the right place at the right time. I happened to be at the Africana Center when scholars such as Michele Wallace, Chandra Mohanty (at Syracuse at the time), and Hortense Spillers were teaching at Cornell. I was able to meet other role models like Hazel Carby, Carole Boyce-Davies and Kimberlé Crenshaw during my tenure there. It was amazing. If there were wavering thoughts about my academic identity, this experience allowed me to fully embrace my role as Black Feminist scholar and discover more about Black Feminist critical thought, such as the work of Ann duCille:

> To claim privileged access to the lives and literature of African American women through what we hold to be the shared experiences of our black female bodies is to cooperate with our own commodification, to buy from and sell back to the dominant culture its constitution of our always already essentialized identity. On the other hand, to relinquish claim to the experiences of the black body and to confirm and affirm its study purely as discourse, simply as a field of inquiry equally open to all, is to collaborate with our own objectification. We become objects of study where we are authorized to be the story but have no special

claim to decoding that story. We can be, but someone else gets to tell us what we mean. (1994:606)

There is another issue that makes understanding the emergence and power of Black Feminism a reality for many women of African descent. The misunderstanding is clearly defined by bell hooks;

> Most people in the United States think of feminism or the more commonly used term 'women's lib' as a movement that aims to make women the social equals of men. This broad definition, popularized by the media and mainstream segments of the movement, raises problematic questions. Since men are not equals in white supremacist, capitalist, patriarchal class structure, which men do women want to be equal to? Do women share a common vision of what equality means? Implicit in this simplistic definition of women's liberation is a dismissal of race and class as factors that, in conjunction with sexism, determine the extent to which an individual will be discriminated against, exploited, or oppressed. (1984:18)

So a challenging aspect of writing the history of Black Feminist thought is to properly place the ideas and events into a constructive context. The myth of universal and collective womanhood is not a realistic history of the feminist movement in the United States. For, even the foundational moments in the movement were fraught with the struggle of what aspect of identity comes first. Do we center on race, sexism or class? The inability of choosing based on an intersectional identity means that to be forced to choose gender over "race" is not always an option for women of color. Therefore, as Patricia Hill Collins so eloquently states, " As a critical social theory, Black feminist thought aims to empower African-American women within the context of social injustice sustained by intersecting oppressions" (2000: 22). So, in an attempt to be inclusive of varying needs and interests, we have to be aware of rhetoric that repositions social inequalities as invisible (Collins 2000). Explained further, Collins warns that against the belief that talking directly about race fosters racism, we shift to a claim of equality that allegedly lies in treating everyone the same (2000:23). This colorblind philosophy further marginalizes the very core of intersectional oppression faced by women of African descent on all fronts.

The history of struggle is a real part of Black Feminist thought in the United States. Although this collective energy can be seen in some ways as exclusionary and even geared toward a particular group of people, the truth is that we as scholars can all learn from the story of Black women's struggles. In Patricia Hill Collins's work, she quotes Katie Cannon's observations, stating that "throughout the history of the United States, the interrelationship of white supremacy and male superiority has characterized the Black woman's reality as a situation of struggle—a struggle to survive in two contradictory worlds simultaneously, one white, privileged, and oppressive, the other black, exploited, and oppressed" ([Cannon 1985:30] in Collins 2000: 26). This perspective puts Black Feminist thought into a wider conversation with all those who are interested in challenging racism, sexism, varying forms of classism and other forms of marginalization and oppression.

Through Black Feminist Archaeology, I bring light to the exclusion of race *and* gender in the analysis of the lives of captive women. I began to clearly see that my questions and methodological approaches were not addressed in the key works and foundational archaeological texts. I felt this challenge was a part of my narrative, but not a story to keep to myself. As Patricia Hill Collins states,

> Being Black and female in the United States continues to expose African-American women to certain common experiences. U. S. Black women's similar work and family experiences as well as our participation in diverse expressions of African-American culture mean that, overall, U. S. Black women as a group live in a different world from that of people who are not Black and female. (2000: 23)

I understood my promotion of a strategically essentialist standpoint in the archaeology of race and gender can possibly be seen as non-inclusive. However, this strategic essentialism has its merits in relation to incorporating a "Black women's collective standpoint" as an integral part of how different responses to classic questions and challenges can highlight and incorporate important aspects of Black women's knowledge (Collins 2000). This collective standpoint can be confusing because it is similar and different simultaneously. The power of this oppositional sameness stands as a testament to the ability of all feminists to engage in the exercise of fighting against intersectional oppression, a dialogue that could be used by any practitioner of archaeology or beyond to enter into an exciting moment of liberation.

As a native New Yorker born in between the hip-hop generation (those born between the years 1965–1984) and what Mark Anthony Neal describes as the "post-soul" era, I can actively trace the development of my connection or disconnection with Black Feminist identity (Kitwana 2002, Morgan 2000, Collins 2006, Neal 2002). So, I am officially a "soul baby" who came to maturity long enough after the Civil Rights Movement and close enough to the conclusion of the Black Power Movement that I can directly relate to how Patricia Hill Collins describes those of us that were coming of age "during a period of initial promise, profound change, and, for far too many, heart-wrenching disappointment" (2006: 3). One characteristic of my childhood was the shift from an overt racial hierarchy of the Jim Crow era [mythically absent in a place like New York City] to a colorblind subtle racism, the new method of marginalization and alienation of my generation (Collins 2006:3). My father was born and raised in Southeast Washington, D.C.; my mother in the Hunts Point section of the South Bronx. They met in Chelsea and lived on Riverside Drive (upper Manhattan) when I was conceived. They didn't stay together for very long, but I began to learn that the expectations they had for me would take me out of New York and allow me to see the world. I traveled all over the continental U. S., went to kindergarden in Taiwan, a little bit of Europe, and traveled to several Caribbean islands and Brazil. Although I was global in perspective, I intimately knew about violence and crime and some of the dirty details of growing up in the Northeast Bronx.

The disconnect between the work of feminists and the concern and needs of the larger Black community was a very real part of my upbringing. So, to not only claim feminism as an identity, but also posit a way to engage in an archaeology that combines Black intellectual thought, Black Feminist thought and anthropological archaeology is taking a chance on many levels. There is an issue of how people of African descent see the disciplines of anthropology and archaeology. There is a trail of racism, sexism and Euro-ethnocentrism clearly associated with the field (LaRoche & Blakey 1999, McClaurin 2001:3). There is often very little exposure to the connection between race, racism, social justice and anthropology through the perspectives of anthropologists of color. However, through sub-fields such as bioarchaeology, medical anthropology, and native ethnography, there has been some incredible work across the globe that addresses the intersectional relationship between race, racism and social justice (for examples see Farmer 2004, Kuwayama 2004, Blakey & Mack 2004, Blakey 1997, Franklin 1997b, Ulysse 2008). There is a space for Black Feminisms in the overall quest for social justice and economic equality, especially across the African Diaspora (including the continent of Africa).

Black feminism and anthropology have already been in dialogue; this reality was fostered by a few intellectual foremothers working their craft for generations. Anthropologists such as Zora Neale Hurston, Vera Green, Irene Diggs, Katherine Dunham, and Caroline Bond Day were among the first to wed issues of race, gender and social commentary in their work. Their toil and effort brought forth generations of Black women scholars who understood the difficulty, but felt the immediate need to push the boundaries of anthropology in a variety of ways. Following in the tradition of these early women, women such as Sheila Walker, Johnetta B. Cole, Beverly Guy-Sheftall, Faye V. Harrison, Angela Gilliam, Gwendolyn Mikell, Lesley Rankin-Hill, Yolanda Moses, Irma McClaurin, A. Lynn Bolles, Theresa Singleton, and Maria Franklin continued to fuse the political and the personal to create a form of Black Feminist Anthropology. Irma McClaurin, editor of *Black Feminist Anthropology*, states:

In positioning itself as an approach derived from but frequently in opposition to mainstream feminist anthropology, Black feminist anthropology becomes a conscious act of knowledge production and canon formation. Despite postmodern critiques of grand theory, master narratives, and canon formation, the reality is that graduate and undergraduate curricula still largely rely upon canonical works in training students. At the same time that Black feminist anthropology constructs its own canon that is both theoretical and based in a politics of praxis and poetics, it seeks to deconstruct the institutionalized racism and sexism that has characterized the history of the discipline of anthropology in the United States and Europe. (2001:1)

These ideas of a formed Black Feminist anthropology in many ways are becoming a part of the way we see the foundational moments of the discipline. And to understand clearly that

Black feminist anthropology is marked by its acknowledgement of theoretical, ideological, and methodological diversity among its practitioners. This is largely because those Black women who dare proclaim themselves feminists draw on the tenets of feminism alongside those of anthropology and embrace an intellectual repertoire that includes women's studies, African American studies, ethnic studies, and African, Caribbean, and Latin American studies. They also embrace the critiques, ideas, metaphors, wisdom, and grounded theories of organic intellectuals in the form of preachers, community activists, street-corner philosophers, and beauty shop therapists alike, who are eloquent about the way in which scholarship has rendered them victims, symbols of poverty, or people without histories. (McClaurin 2001:3)

So, for this hip-hop generational soul baby, Black feminism, although initially hard to claim, became the means for my participation in Black Feminists' struggles all over the world. The needs of that community, and a connection to one of the central tenets written so long ago by the Combahee River Collective, "If Black women were free, it would mean that everyone else would have to be free since our freedom would necessitate the destruction of all the systems of oppression (1982)," forged the final point to my commitment to a lifetime in the struggle for social and political justice for people of African descent and against forms of oppression and discrimination throughout the world from a firmly accepted Black Feminist identity (Combahee River Collective 1982).

Black Feminist Archaeology in Theory and Praxis

Margaret Conkey describes the ambivalence that archaeology has toward "doing theory" in her article mentioned earlier, "Questioning Theory: Is There a Gender to Theory in Archaeology" (2007). This ambivalence toward theory often falls into two categories: on one side is the empiricist approach that avoids any interpretive work beyond the empirical "fact." Then, on the other side of this camp is the process of contextualizing archaeological data as both cultural and historical material that is directly connected to "speculative modes of inquiry and engage with imaginative theoretical constructs" ([Wylie 1981] in Conkey 2007). Conkey then points out that feminist interventions have shown a "strategic ambivalence" toward doing theory or not doing theory, for theory in many ways is masculinized and unmarked as such because of the "ideological control of the society at large" (Conkey 2007:289). She continues to distinguish some of the differences that a feminist perspective brings to the use of theory in archaeology:

> On the other hand, there is a very different way to think of theory, a view much more compatible with feminist perspectives and much more suited, in fact, to the nature of most archaeological inquiry. There is a view of theory as revelatory, as opening up new spaces, as challenging assumptions so as to 'conceive of our own thinking... in new ways'.... The nature of theory, by this account, is 'to undo, through a contesting of postulates and premises, what you thought you knew.' (Conkey 2007: 297)

One of the key components of Black Feminist Archaeology is to use the tools in my discipline to shape and enhance the stories of people of African descent in the past, present and future. I then connect the history and circumstances that inspired my invisibility as a part of the methodological challenges. This healing process was again linked to forms of scholarship and inquiry normally outside of archaeological interpretation; namely, Black Feminist thought. So, it is essential to properly place this methodological tradition at the center of Black Feminist Archaeology. Part of the motivation behind the formation of the various forms of Black Feminism is directly linked to the "distinctive set of social practices that accompany our [women of African descent] particular history within a unique matrix of domination characterized by intersecting oppressions" (Collins 2000: 23). This unique set of circumstances is what makes this theoretical perspective to address the multivalent forms of institutional, structural and individual oppression. Black Feminist thought arises from the need for women of African descent to write about ourselves, to provide "a much needed awareness about the lives, relationships, families, environments, stresses and strategies involved with the survival of this population in the United States" (Burgess & Brown 2000:1). I was very disappointed in the methods provided by the discipline of history to answer the deeper questions I had about myself.

> The exclusionary practices of women who dominate feminist discourse have made it practically impossible for new and varied theories to emerge. Feminism has its party line and women who feel a need for a different strategy, a different foundation, often find themselves ostracized and silenced…. Yet groups of women who feel excluded from feminist discourse and praxis can make a place for themselves only if they first create, via critiques, an awareness of the factors that alienate them. (hooks 2000: 9)

A Black Feminist Archaeology takes its initial cue from Black Feminist Anthropology; however, instead of combining Black intellectual thought and feminist theory, we also add archaeological theory to create a purposefully coarse and textured analytical framework. The hope here is to create compelling questions, take nothing for granted and always understand your own position as researcher in the overall scheme. In many ways, historical archaeology has been described as a field that has the potential to enhance the study of the African American past (see Harrison 1999, Orser 1998b). The question remains, have we been successful in this mission. The stakes are extremely high and the odds are often not in our favor. As Paul Mullins describes, "Muddy definitions of diasporan identity and equivocal analysis of race have not always clearly positioned archaeology in antiracial discourses; historical archaeology uneasily negotiates between African anti-essentialism and the evidence for African cultural persistence" (2008: 104).

In the late 1930s there was an archaeological project just outside of Savannah, Georgia. The site was Irene Mound. This site was excavated, analyzed and interpreted almost completely by women (Claassen 1999). Although women were not chosen for leadership roles, they analyzed artifacts, worked on archaeological drawings, and assisted with the site reports and other interpretation. The irony of this site is that at this time Euroamerican women were discouraged from doing fieldwork in the United States. While more than eighty-seven women of African descent were clearing trees, removing stumps, hauling dirt with heavy equipment, and excavating the site (Claassen 1999). From October 1937 through January 1940, a crew of 117 people, all personnel for the Worker Progress Administration (WPA), were a part of this moment in history. This was one of the first examples in the United States of women of African descent doing archaeology. Now, this seems exciting, but this was not an ideal job for several reasons. Even knowing this, when I first saw the pictures of the women of Irene Mound, I smiled. This meant that there was proof, I was not alone, and it was humbling in many ways. I saw these women, in their long dresses and sun hats, toiling in the soil and realizing that their efforts would not lead to careers in archaeology. The work that the Irene Mound women were engaged in was perceived as just heavy labor, testimony to the continuum of the type of work that women of African descent had always done. However, there was still a brief moment where I felt proud to see women that looked like me engaged in real archaeology.

As I turned the pages of Cheryl Claassen's incredible article I was increasingly amazed at how restrictive field work was for Euroamerican

Figure 1.1: African American women excavating at Irene Mound.
(Photo courtesy of Georgia Historical Society.)

women at this historic moment. In the late 1930s the WPA was still
trying to determine the appropriate types of work for women and men
of African descent. For the most part, the work for poor women, regard-
less of race, included renovating and repairing clothing and household
articles, domestic service, caring for the sick, cooking in soup kitchens,
and sewing (Claassen 1999). In the spring of 1936, a pilot project was
"set up by WPA authorities to employ thirty to forty Negro women
as an archaeological field crew under white supervisors trained by A.
R. Kelly and J. A. Ford" (Claassen 1991:95). The site was Swift Creek,
and the experiment worked; therefore additional sites were proposed,
eventually leading to the Irene Mound site.

This was initially a shock, but not all that surprising. It did provide a moment of clarity in thinking critically about the work that I
do and the opportunity as a woman of African descent to engage in
the world of Americanist archaeology. Black Feminist Archaeology is

a method that centers the intersectionality of race, gender, and class into a larger discussion of archaeological approaches to interpreting the American past. This theory takes into account the disadvantage of how these aspects of identity (primarily race and gender) act as a doubled (and with class a triple) form of oppression. This theory also considers the direct connection of the past with contemporary issues of racism and sexism in ways that allow researchers to see how the past influences and shapes contemporary society and perhaps forces us all to be more sensitive to the larger implications of our research. Black Feminist Archaeology used in the field could potentially add more dimension to the questions asked of the physical site, the approaches to excavation, the interpretation of artifacts, stories of the people who occupied these historic sites, and the conversations we have with stakeholders.

For those who are conducting research, how has race or racism factored into who becomes an archaeologist, who trains archaeologists, and who become the principle investigators for projects of all sizes (Franklin 1997b, McKee 1995, Blakey 1997, Paynter 2001, Agbe-Davies 2003)? Archaeology as a discipline still does not capture excitement among people of African descent. Archaeology still appears to be exclusionary to the African descendent community on a variety of levels. The popular imagery of the "Indiana Jones factor" has never related to me as a woman of African descent, nor does it capture a lot of clout with my home community. The value of what I do and the tools I use is still not a part of the larger quest to achieve social and political justice. Spending time at Cornell's Africana Studies and Research Center, I quickly realized that anthropology and archaeology were not viewed as beneficial to contemporary struggles and issues among people of the African Diaspora. It can be difficult for people of African descent to see the value of archaeology, because they have never seen themselves reflected in the makeup of the practitioners or in those being served by the outcome of the research agendas.

Changing the way that historical archaeology is viewed outside of the discipline is a central part of Black Feminist Archaeology.

Black Feminist Archaeology also proposes a theoretical approach that is not as heavily influenced by the interpretation of material culture, but that looks more critically at the theories and ideas that are often neglected by constraints of a strict material analysis. The questions generated during the process of forming research agendas can combine traditional archaeological research methods with our work within the communities associated with historic sites. The public archaeology becomes an engaged and activist archaeology when there is a connection between the archaeological methods and issues important to contemporary communities. The agendas and research initiatives are shared and talked about in ways that are rare in academic climates, but essential for moving toward an archaeology of relevance and inclusion so many archaeologists view as a positive direction for the discipline (see also Agbe-Davies 2010, McDavid 1997, Little & Shackel 2007, Mullins 2008, LaRoche & Blakey 1997, Perry & Blakey 1997, Parker 1991).

Within Black Feminist Archaeology is an emphasis on the cultural landscape and the importance of how the use and meaning of space is directly connected to culture and people. This philosophy has persisted in how I incorporate the environment with an enhanced understanding of how people live in a place and what these details can tell us about their everyday struggles and triumphs. Artifacts are never just material; they mean more than broken pieces of people's lives buried in the ground. These items provide another dimension to the written word, which is part of the strength of what archaeologists do. Artifacts can possibly bring forth elements of a more interesting story to communities that would traditionally never see themselves connected with or interested in archaeology as a part of understanding their collective pasts.

As archaeology will teach us throughout this book, the written text is full of assumptions that are often contradictory to the lived truth. Whether that be individuals that have historically been considered poor, but were materially wealthy, or captive Africans creating and maintaining spaces of autonomy in full view of those in power, archaeology often provides an alternative view of spaces, place and sites of cultural production. These are the very strengths that quickly turned my attention from a reliance on the documentary record to an eclectic combination of literature, artifacts, and cultural landscape to explore the incredible possibilities of material analysis.

There are several themes that tie this book together. I discuss three key sites to demonstrate how Black Feminist Archaeology can enhance our overall understanding of the African American past and how African Diaspora archaeology can be beneficial to a variety of disciplines. The first theme is that of the household or homeplace. I recognize how this has been classically used as a tool for disenfranchisement, separation, or "Othering"; however, in this case, a deeper understanding of the Black domestic sphere is a source of information, strength, and cultural capital. The next theme is that of material wealth versus class distinctions and social poverty. I address the assumption of how the Black domestic sphere becomes a tool to promote a very early version of a culture of poverty model by ignoring the very presence of material wealth excavated at sites of people of African descent. Lastly, I look at labor—more specifically, women's labor and women's choice. I explore the ways in which women who were maintaining the houses and lifestyles of the Victorian aesthetic (by cleaning houses, taking in sewing, doing laundry, raising children and cooking food) created their own spaces of comfort and family pride. The consumer choices made by people of African descent is an interesting way to understand a little of what life was like in a racialized nineteenth-century world. The action of buying, trading or keeping things is a universal practice. This may allow for people who have not really used archaeology directly to understand its contributions as a grassroots approach to understanding material and space together; to examine how women, for example, used certain spaces as sites of their own as a form of cultural production. All these factors revolve around home, material, and cultural choice, factors that can directly be seen accompanying other disciplines and contemporary issues of historical memory and a collective understanding of the past.

CHAPTER II

The Hermitage

Going to Church

It was early Tuesday morning and we were back in the field after our quick weekend break. At this point in the season I was beginning to feel the finality of the dwindling summer. I knew it was time to assess what had been done and what needed to be finished before it was time to pack up and go. The air was cool and the morning was relaxed and calm. That is when Mary, a public school teacher from Boston and a volunteer with EarthWatch, started a quiet conversation with me about her weekend adventures. Mary was a member of an African Methodist Episcopalian (AME) church in Boston and looked in the phone book to find a church to attend during her two week stay in Tennessee. Scott's Hollow AME Zion Church was less than five miles away from the Hermitage. She told me that her visit was incredible; the people there were excited about her visiting from Boston (and the Hermitage) and happy to hear about the type of work that was going on. She also brought my name up, and they wanted to meet me next Sunday. It was at that point that they began to describe a rich history of African descent people in the area. Church members shared stories of local family connections and the close relationships of the other African American churches in the Hermitage area. As she continued talking, I felt the hair on the back of my neck stand on end. Emotions hit me like a ton of bricks. I felt like I wanted to cry. It was as if in that moment, I had learned of some long, lost friend that had been missing from my life for years and that Mary was the person who would bring us together again. It was not a feeling of a research breakthrough or a means to start a community history project; it felt more like for the first time since I had arrived that I was not the only African person around. I felt overwhelmed. I listened intently as Mary spoke. Then she told me about Stateland Baptist Church. It was located across the road from the Hermitage and was a symbol of the relationship between the plantation and the all Black neighborhood that had been there for generations. We made plans to go to Stateland immediately after the day was over—no shower, no relaxing, just a quick drive across the road to see what we could find. My mind raced and raced as I tried to concentrate on my field notes and other duties, but I remained anxious and on edge. I had little to say to most of the crew that entire day. I was hurt, I was shocked, I had feelings of guilt and shame for not knowing (or looking for) the African American community. The day was over, and we hopped into my Jeep and bounced over to the Stateland neighborhood. The first thing we stumbled upon was a small cemetery that had old gravestones. As we stood there in our dirty, dusty attire and tried to read some of the headstones, a tiny, loud white dog began to bark ferociously. The the door of the house next to the cemetery opened, and an elderly woman came to the steps to see who we were and what we were doing so close to her house. That marked the first time I met Mrs. Minerva (Jackson) Washington; a relationship that became one that I will never forget. I spent many Saturday mornings with Mrs. Washington. I got to know what it was like to be of African descent in a place like the Hermitage; the history of discrimination. And it was Mrs. Washington that helped me to meet many more local community members. I attended a few church services, family barbecues, and other informal interviews. This was all to just figure out what this place was and what it meant to the Black people who lived around the museum. Those conversations changed the way I saw the work I was doing on the site on a daily basis, but it also gave me the strength to continue when being at the Hermitage got difficult. It allowed me to escape the details of archaeology and talk to people about what life was like everyday in a small suburb of Nashville, Tennessee.

Note: I have to thank the people that invited me into their homes, that allowed me to ask what often seemed like silly questions, and allowed me to figure out why I was at a place like the Hermitage. There are many people who influenced many of my thoughts and understandings of the history of the site and ancestors that called that plantation home. Many of these friendships will continue to be private and separate from my work, but I will always have a place for them in my heart and my mind. I thank you, too. And last, I want to say a special thank you to Mrs. Minerva Washington, who is no longer on this side; may her stories continue to spice up how I see the South and my place in it.

Introduction

My first thoughts about forming a Black Feminist framework for historical archaeology came in the midst of my dissertation fieldwork at the First Hermitage Site on Andrew Jackson's Hermitage Plantation. In 1997, when the project began, I was focused on doing good and meaningful archaeology. This meant removing material from the ground and going through the archaeological process in a careful and thoughtful way. Initially, we knew where we wanted to focus our excavations, so we mapped our target areas, created a plan of action and laid down an excavation grid. The next steps included digging, discovery and adjustment. We then excavated stratigraphically, digging one layer at a time to reveal how each artifact relates to each other and the particular layer in which it was found. This can be challenging because it changes daily, depending on what you find or do not find. We remove each artifact and place it in a bag with the proper label, identify and catalog each artifact, and then catalog these items into a computer database to be interpreted later.

When an artifact is removed from the ground, it is changed forever. It is permanently removed from its surroundings or context, and therefore becomes an individual item until it is placed in association with another related object. It is then the job of the archaeologist to use particular tools and strategies to understand how each piece of material is related to each other. This process seems straightforward; however, there is also a more fine-tuned understanding of the site, its inhabitants and how that material may relate to the people who used each item. When certain artifacts are found together, the meaning of these artifacts can change (Brown & Cooper 1990, Smith 1977, Samford 1995, Perry & Woodruff 2003, Russell 1997, McKee 1995, Wilkie 2003, Fennel 2007, Battle 2007b). These factors were constants in the back of my mind, but my main focus was on the business of archaeology. Everything had to be done right. As my first excavation season unfolded, my ideas and questions became more fine-tuned; they became more focused on aspects of life I had not thought about when I started excavating any given unit.

I took my time excavating and thought critically about how each future move would impact possible research changes. My original research design focused exclusively on exterior areas of the First Hermitage Site, specifically the yard area between the Jackson Farmhouse and the Kitchen Quarter (see Figure 2.3). I felt that my efforts to understand the daily activities through archaeology would be best served by concentrating on this particular location. Slowly, I began to recognize the Hermitage project as more than digging and following the direction the artifacts took us. I had to combine practice and theory in ways that at first I found intimidating. Although it was very important to let the artifacts take the lead, I had to listen to the developing narrative of the people that used the material that was coming together as the artifacts came out of the ground. I found that with this approach, I was developing a methodogy that could highlight a complex web of inquiry that could lead to different types of answers to my original questions. In other words, my approach essentially started with the artifact, but also recognized much of the story related to captive people and not just their material remains.

As a trained historian, I had always subconsciously seen the identity of the "slave" as masculine (White 1999, Patton 1999, Davis

1981, Morton 1991). As my time in the academy progressed, I recognized very similar frustrations I had felt in my personal intellectual development manifested in the type of research I was engaging with. These frustrations were among the several reasons behind my transition from history to anthropology. To find a way to challenge the sexual erasure of slavery, reflect my passions, and figure out how to use archaeology to interpret the past differently was a top priority. At the Hermitage, I knew that I could shape the site to be more than just another example of plantation archaeology; there was a potential of telling a realistic and compelling story of gender, captivity and domestic life. This was harder than I had imagined because at many moments in the overall process I was thinking through my own personal and scholarly development. As mentioned before, this was at the beginning stages of developing my own Black Feminist identity formation, where I was forcing myself to mold a feminism that was compatible with my archaeological work.

So, I can now write this chapter as a Black feminist who came to understand her place in the world of post-contact Americanist archaeology and made it work. So my later analysis, using a Black Feminist Archaeology, is thinking through my work after excavations have been completed. My methodological approach was in its infancy; however, it was not just a way of asking slightly different questions, but a means of figuring out ways to posit a dialogue that could be useful in the past, present, and future—to archaeologists and beyond. Through my analysis I will illustrate how a site's interpretation can change over time. This is what has happened in my relationship with the Hermitage Museum and my understanding of the archaeological project I was involved in over ten years ago.

The Hermitage Plantation

The Hermitage Plantation is a historical museum that opened for tours in 1889. It was the plantation home of Andrew Jackson, a major public figure in the history of the United States. As the seventh president of the United States, he is remembered as the stoic and unmovable "Old Hickory," hero of New Orleans, the architect of Indian removal, and the father of Jacksonian Democracy. There are volumes written adding to the legend of Andrew Jackson, filled with stories of humble beginnings and controversial political moves. Yet, Jackson was also the enslaver of more than 160 captive Africans and the proprietor of a 1,120 acre plantation in Middle Tennessee. The myth of Jackson as the first "common man" president was not possible without the work of captive labor, who guaranteed his wealth and prosperity.

John Frost captures how Andrew Jackson was remembered later in life:

> Long in retirement, devoted to rural occupations, disconnected with the strife of party politics, and in familiar intercourse with the sons of those pioneers, who had conquered a rude wilderness to the hand of cultivation, he learned to value the strong sense of freedom, the bold intellect and hardy virtues of an agricultural people, and to perceive that the perpetuity of our free institutions depends on the continuance of their virtue and intelligence. (1861:485)

Andrew Jackson, however, was very much a man of his time. A lawyer, politician, statesman and later president, he was a complex individual to say the least. He had a profound hatred of the British, which stemmed from his childhood and his blaming the British for the deaths of his parents. This hatred translated into an obsessive patriotism and a hard edge that existed in all aspects of his adult life. He had no problems with the idea of enslaving another human being, yet the constant growth of his captive population was often attributed by his contemporaries as overindulgence (Battle 2004). In my opinion, his true quality was his acute sense of plantation management and the manipulation of people. The more humane he is said to have treated his captive laborers, the better chance he saw this as a mechanism for maintaining certain levels of crop production, economic efficiency, and the fullest plantation yields possible.

The Hermitage exhibit is set to reflect the household in 1834, when Jackson returned from eight years serving in the White House. The Hermitage was his home from 1804 until his death in 1845.

Figure 2.1
An engraving of
the Hermitage
Mansion
as it appeared
in the 1830s.
(Photo courtesy
of the Hermitage
Museum.)

After Jackson's death, his adopted son, Andrew Jr., inherited the plantation. The family no longer prospered as they had while Jackson was alive. After several attempts to manage the plantation, find alternative crops, and begin new plantation ventures elsewhere, the family under Andrew Jr. was forced to sell parts of the property starting in the 1850s and then ultimately the mansion and immediate outbuildings to the state of Tennessee. In the mid to late 1880s a group of wealthy and influential Nashvillian women formed the Ladies' Hermitage Association (LHA), which sought to save the property from complete destruction and assumed responsibility of the mansion and the immediate surrounding area. The offical opening of the mansion to the public was on July 17, 1889 (Doris 1915). The Hermitage Museum today is a park-like setting dedicated to the story of Andrew Jackson and the many complexities of plantation life. The organization has focused on preserving the legacy of the Jackson family before the mansion and surrounding land went into complete decay due to years of neglect. The Hermitage museum now consists of the Andrew Jackson Center (which contains the museum, a gift shop, and an auditorium), Jackson's Greek revival mansion, and several buildings located on the original 1,120 acres.

A Long Archaeological Legacy

For over thirty years archaeology has been a part of the Hermitage plantation. A majority of these excavations centered on structure alterations and building construction projects on the museum property. The earliest archaeological excavations were sponsored by the LHA and the Tennessee American Revolution Bicentennial Commission in 1974 and were dedicated to exploring the standing structures of the First Hermitage Site (Smith 1977). The First Hermitage Site was significant because it was the home of Andrew and Rachel Jackson from 1804–1821. It was where Rachel Donelson Jackson spent most of her time at the plantation; she only lived in the larger, brick mansion for a few years before her death. Therefore, the First Hermitage served as a symbol of Jackson's humble beginnings, and a majority of the archaeology was focused on finding information about the site to create a master plan for better understanding the early days of Jackson's tenure on the property. These initial excavations focused on outbuildings and the working plantation, which eventually led to archaeologists shifting the focus toward the captive African population (Thomas 1998).

Between 1970 and 1980 archaeologists began to spread out and investigate other areas of the property. These early projects laid the foundation for questions that would be revised in later years. In 1989 the museum made the commitment to begin a full-time archaeology program and appointed Dr. Larry McKee as director. The new archaeology program was created at a moment when plantation and African American archaeology were expanding from the search for "African patterns" to thinking about more complicated questions and larger cultural issues of captive peoples across the colonial and antebellum landscapes [including the Caribbean] (Singleton & Bograd 1995, Franklin 1997a). For more than twelve years, McKee's archaeology program also hosted one of the most sought after archaeological internships of the moment. It was a five-week program that included excavating, artifact processing, some interpretation, reading and a chance to experience "real" archeology. This included living in a crew house, sharing meals, getting up before the break of day (not exciting for me), and experiencing the finer points of what Nashville had to offer. During these years three distinct residential areas were explored (see Figure 2.2). The

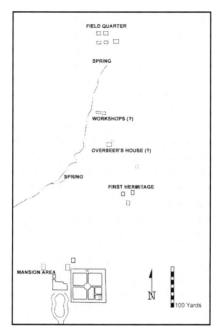

Figure 2.2: Map of archaeological areas investigated between 1989 and 2000. (Illustration courtesy of Jamie Brandon.)

Mansion Backyard, immediately behind the mansion; the First Hermitage Site, about 250 yards northeast of the mansion; and the Field Quarter Site, which was located more than 500 yards from the mansion and close to main cotton fields (Thomas 1995, 1998, McKee 1995, Russell 1997, McKee & Galle 2000, Battle 2004).

My dissertation fieldwork focused on the First Hermitage area from 1997– 2001. Previous archaeology at the site was conducted sporadically between 1975 and 1980. The excavations were usually related to maintenance on the First Hermitage structures or brief explorations of possible locations of other outbuildings related to the early years of the plantation (Smith 1977, Hinshaw 1979, Galle & McKee 2000). There was a long history of the LHA using a variety of methods to maintain the First Hermitage cabins, from innovative ways of making the site attractive to visitors, creating various walkways and paths, or hosting outdoor garden parties and other events. These structures were also used as storage and even as temporary housing for prison workers working on the local roads. All of which offered us interesting challenges archaeologically. As excavations began, there were several days where we would find pieces of chewing gum, Kodak flash bulbs, and coins that spanned the decades. This I quickly learned was a part of archaeology at a one hundred year old museum I had never thought about.

There are varying accounts of the property's appearance during the early stages of Jackson's occupation (one example is from Parton 1850). The history of the Hermitage begins when Middle Tennessee was still considered a frontier. Although constantly active in the political and social scene of the developing city of Nashville, Jackson was content with his various pursuits. "At first it had not been his intention to settle permanently in the western wilderness but he was such an immediate success as a frontier lawyer that he changed his mind" (Remini 1998a:45). When Andrew Jackson first moved to the property in 1804, the initial motivation was to live out his days with Rachel, pay off his debts, and recover from recent financial misfortune (Remini 1977:132). Involved in several business ventures, Jackson as a merchant sold coffee, rum, gunpowder, and "occasionally engaged in slave trading as a service for a friend or client" (Remini 1977:133). Jackson never stuck to his original plan; instead, he decided to delve into local politics, which then led to his rise to national prominence. The year 1821 marked a profound restructuring of the entire plantation (McKee & Galle 2000, Jones 2002, Battle 2004). In 1820 Jackson sold his Alabama plantation and moved a majority of the captive workers to the Hermitage, increasing the population from approximately forty to eighty people (Jones 2002). Cotton became the cash crop of the plantation, and Jackson had the labor force to support the plantation's growing needs. 1821 was also the year the brick Great House was completed. This property began to reflect the man that Jackson was becoming, both politically and financially. The plantation went from a self-sustaining small farm with a few families to a gentleman's estate of more than 1,000 acres of land and an abundance of cotton, livestock and other crops that were all labor dependent. Jackson's absence after 1828, when he left for the White House, had a profound effect on the captive African population (Battle 2004).

From afar, Jackson tried to manage the firing of abusive overseers, maintain a sense of order through Andrew Jackson Jr.'s poor plantation management, and see to the larger issues of plantation workers. It was during this time that the captive population pulled together and leaned on the strength of extended families and kinship circles to maintain a semblance of order, stability, and safety.

Focus on the First Hermitage Site began in 1996, the year I arrived at the Hermitage as an intern. There was an extensive field survey at the site to determine the plan of action for the 1997 season (Galle & McKee 2000, Thomas 199). When excavations began there were only two log structures standing (see Figure 2.3). The Farm House was a two-story log structure that served as the main house for the Jackson family from 1804–1821 (Remini 1977, McKee & Galle 2000, Jones 2002). The Kitchen Quarter was built around 1805 and served as a kitchen and quarter dwelling during the Jackson period (Brigance 1975, Smith 1976, Jones 2002). Located about forty feet east of the Jackson Farmhouse, the Kitchen Quarter was a log duplex with two end chimneys measuring roughly twenty by forty feet (McKee & Galle 2000). The excavated areas of the First Hermitage Site included structural remains of the Southeast and South Cabins (see Figure 2.3), the interiors of both standing structures (the Kitchen Quarter and the Jackson Farmhouse), and areas surrounding the buildings referred to here as "yard areas."

One of the three main focuses of the site was the Kitchen Quarter, located just east of the Jackson Farmhouse (see Figure 2.3). According to oral histories and visitors' accounts (Parton 1850, Dorris 1915, Brigance 1975) this structure served as a central meeting point for the captive community in the early years of the Hermitage farm. The Kitchen Quarter and the immediate surrounding area proved one of the most significant lines of evidence for addressing my questions. It held a majority of the features that are associated with the various domestic activities of the First Hermitage community. From the beginning of the site's occupation, this seemed to be a central meeting place, especially because of the location of the main kitchen, one of the original double-pen structures. Its lengthy occupation was by

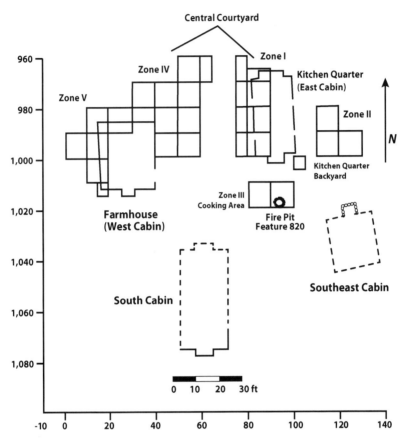

Figure 2.3: Map of First Hermitage archaeology, including positions of Jackson Farmhouse and Kitchen Quarter. (Illustration courtesy of Maria Franklin.)

far the most stable and most likely reflective of several generations of captive families. For all of these reasons excavation units were placed on three of the four sides surrounding the structure (see Figure 2.3). The second focus was the Jackson Farmhouse, which revealed a complicated history that included the alteration of the dwelling and use as a local landmark symbolizing Andrew Jackson's humble beginnings. Finally, the third focus was the yard area. The general approach to this part of the site was to look for distinct architectural features and indications of past activities when the property was a farm and small quartering area. As excavations continued, the technique was altered to accommodate what we found and what we did not. This led to shifting from excavating large ten by ten foot excavation units into smaller areas across the site.

As research at the Hermitage shifted from data recovery to data analysis, the first step was to place the material in proper chronological order. The period of active occupation at the plantation, essentially the entire nineteenth century, was a time of tremendous change both at the local and broader regional contexts (McKee 1995). The artifact assemblages represented successive periods of pioneer establishment, the classic cotton plantation economy, the Hermitage's economic decline, and the extraordinary changes brought by the Civil War and emancipation (McKee 1995).

The Functional Plantation Model

As I began to think about the structure and shape of the plantation landscape, I wanted to fully grasp why it was so difficult to articulate a possible scenario of how the captive community viewed their immediate environment. It was years later, as I continued to think about cultural landscapes, resistance, *habitus*, and historical silences that I formed what I call a *functional plantation model*. This theory, worked through after my dissertation research, is an example of how I see Black Feminist Archaeology moving beyond the obvious interpretive borders and including neglected ways of seeing plantation life. Away from the physical landscape, but deep in thought about how the landscape functioned, I considered possible meanings behind the placement of things and then placement in general.

An important aspect of archaeological interpretation is considering how landscapes can reflect the needs of inhabitants. By using Black Feminist Archaeology, the emphasis falls more on the cultural formation processes, defined more concretely as the processes of human behavior that affect or transform artifacts after their initial period of use in a given activity (Schiffer 1987). At the First Hermitage, I was examining a compact sequence of events that had to be fleshed out to figure out how the cultural landscape was transformed from one period to another. In looking further, I decided to also think about the impact of material on places they were found and places where no artifacts were discovered. The absence of material being as important as their presence.

Artifacts are not neutral when they are recovered from the archaeological record. Although every artifact has a life history that is unique in some respects, certain recurrent activities and processes crosscut all life histories and make it possible to generalize about stages related to the use of artifacts in the systemic context (Schiffer 1972). At the First Hermitage Site, it was not important to determine who particular artifacts belonged to. Instead, the research questions focused on how these artifacts illustrated the transformation of space in culturally significant ways for captive Africans living at the site from 1804 to 1850.

In post-contact archaeology we now understand that artifacts can potentially tell us small aspects of the lifeways and beliefs of the people who used them (Brown & Cooper 1990, Leone & Fry 1999). When excavating sites occupied by captive Africans, there are several approaches to consider. At the Hermitage, I had the unique opportunity of knowing exactly where most of the structures stood, how the quarter was basically organized, and a general idea of the documented history with basic information about the operating plantation during the antebellum period.

As I moved beyond my dissertation years, I thought through what the cultural landscape of a plantation looked like theoretically. So, my functional plantation model was a slow and interesting process that I outline here.

The Plantation Proper

The first realm in my functional plantation model is made up of the plantation whole, including all of its environs (meaning non-cultivated and unoccupied spaces). This realm is the first step in how I organized my understanding of the functional aspects of something as large as a plantation. I wanted to consider how the plantation operated as a distinct entity. Jackson wanted his plantation to be self-sufficient, consistently productive, and able to sustain itself through lean times (Battle 2004). He envisioned a place where everything would be produced and manufactured on site. His goal was to return home from the White House and fall immediately into his role as Gentleman Farmer.

Cotton was the cash crop of the plantation, but there were a variety of other yields such as: wheat, hemp, the kitchen garden, gardens planted by captive people, a cotton gin and press, corn, horses (including thoroughbreds), cattle, chickens, guinea hens, pigs; and a race track (Battle 2004). This meant that work was done year round and there were always tasks to be completed, building projects to continue, crops to maintain, and animals to attend. There was also an interesting social exchange between the many people that kept the plantation running. These social networks made up the first realm of captive life. This realm is usually the surface phase of analysis, what is often considered plantation life as a whole. However, although this is an extremely important level of analysis, I used Black Feminist Archaeology to consider the spaces that remain hidden in plain "site." I wanted to include the socialization process in the private spaces that were often characterized as meaningless exchanges to outsiders, but were essential to Black cultural production (Bourdieu 1977, Wilkie 2000, Battle-Baptiste 2007a).

The Captive African Domestic Sphere

The second realm was the captive domestic sphere. This area has a multitude of meanings for the occupants. It becomes the center for life, culture, tradition, and humanity. The domestic sphere has an "exaggerated importance" for the captive community (Davis 1981, White 1999, Battle-Baptiste 2007a, Young 2004, Wilkie 2000, Edwards 1998). It was one of the few places where captive women and men could gain their humanity and maintain and nurture their families (Davis 1981; Battle-Baptiste 2004, 2007a; hooks 1990; White 1999; Wilkie 2000; Young 2004).

The quarter was under the "jurisdiction" of the enslaver, but never fully controlled by him. Each plantation was different. On some properties it was important to know exactly what was going on every moment of the captive laborer's day. This was not the case for the Jackson property. Much of what happened at the quarters was not considered top priority. There was no direct evidence that Jackson needed to account for each hour of the laborer's day. This was mostly the responsibility of the overseer; the details were not as important for the enslaver, especially one that was frequently absent like Jackson. As an absentee landowner, he needed to be informed on matters that would concern him in the long term, decisions, financial matters, or large problems with laborers or escapees, not the everyday management tasks.

The captive African domestic sphere became increasingly significant as I began to focus in on an analysis of captive women. The domestic realm, also known as the realm of women, is a "taken for granted" place. My analysis pushes for the insertion of race in the overall understanding of the plantation domestic sphere. Captive women were not subject to the virtues and limitations of Euroamerican women or Victorian mores of the time (Davis 1981, Patton 1999, White 1999, Wilkie 2000, Bush 1990). Therefore, to equate the captive domestic sphere as the central domain of women is limiting for the overall analysis. The reality that their domestic sphere reached beyond four walls of a structure, and so this realm consisted of inside, outside, around, and between various quartering areas, depending on the size of the plantation. So, by using a Black Feminist Archaeological analysis, I developed a different line of questioning about the roles of women and the "home." The domestic realm was not the sole concern of captive women; there was a necessity for shared domestic labor in the quarters, and each member of the community shared in everyday chores and responsibilities. Issues of childcare, food preparation, household upkeep and maintaining domestic and personal relationships were matters that non-captive women did not have to consider in the same ways.

....

The Labor Sphere

The third realm of the model was the labor sphere or work spaces. These are agricultural lands, curing houses, corn cribs, stables, blacksmith shops, the cotton gin and press. Using the lens of Black Feminist Archaeology, I compared how these work areas relate to the plantation and the central domestic sphere, and visa versa. I admit, work spaces were in the background and never took full shape in my dissertation. I continue to have difficulty trying to articulate how to interpret these spaces, based on the lack of archaeological work we did on these portions of the larger Hermitage project (there were excavations on the Triplex Quarters in 1996 and the Cotton Gin in 2001). Work spaces force us to think in new ways about labor issues; labor factored so much within the realm of slavery. This would be a good place to have statistics about the work load and the responsibility of captive women, men and children on particular plantations. Looking at the labor sphere would also be directly connected to the first realm, the entire plantation. There is a process to how we do work, a socialization, a collective response to harsh and excessive workloads. The added factor is that Jackson owned one of the two cotton gin and presses in Davidson County; therefore surrounding plantations would often bring raw cotton to the Hermitage to process further, making for constant and temporary fluxes of captives from other plantations. These exchanges would likely have taken place in the labor sphere more than any other location on the property. Captive Africans were defined by the work they did, which also made work in many ways a key to gender equalization. This also made this realm a very important factor in plantation life; however, one often neglected in the archaeology of quarter areas and mansions. Therefore, this realm would also be a very compelling discussion for archaeology to take further.

The Wilderness

The fourth realm was the wilderness. The untamed space that was often used as a place of retrieval, to regroup, escape, hide, worship, hunt, gather medicinal herbs or travel. This space has been neglected and misunderstood by historians and archaeologists as an important realm of understanding the lives of captive Africans. This is where literature in many ways provided an interesting glimpse into complicated themes and ideas I knew of in other aspects of my life, but wanted to bring into my archaeological work. K. Zauditu-Salassie describes aspects of these themes, "In her third novel, *Tar Baby* (1981), Toni Morrison inscribes indigenous knowledge, representing physical and cultural landscapes as sites of power to balance individuals and restore community cohesion" (2009:97). For me, the wilderness is one of the most exciting aspects of understanding how the plantation functioned for captive peoples. These in-between places were always spaces where captive peoples navigated no matter what region or period. This is how captive people maintained abroad marriages and used the environment to trade, visit, and worship. This space also symbolizes the second most important place to find solace and remove oneself from the daily rigors of captivity. Those who had knowledge of herbs and medicines had an intimate relationship with the untamed spaces between plantations. This untamed space was used by all members of the captive community. We know this through sources in history and archaeology. For example, Laurie Wilkie describes the intimate knowledge of midwives pre- and post-emancipation, and the use of powerful herbs such as "Pennyroyal, ergot, tanxy, cotton, and rue, abortifacients that had been used for centuries" (2003: 150).

So, the need to expand the limited notion of tamed and untamed in many ways undermines the complexity of these in-between spaces. Another way to think about this fourth realm is to relate it to the ways that self liberated (Maroon) communities understood these "untamed" spaces (Weik 1997). The spiritual realm includes how we understand the varying functions of these active yardscapes and teases out how these spaces served the needs of the living and the dead (Heath & Bennett 2000:39). In Indigenous African traditions, there has always been a strong emphasis on remembering those who lived before. For captive communities, previous generations provided stories and lessons that then shaped the needs of contemporary successive generations.

It was this spiritual connection that remained beneath the radars of Eurocentric modes of behavior and understanding. So this is also why the act of sweeping was so important in my interpretation of the Central Courtyard. It was, as Barbara Heath and Amber Bennett explain, an ordinary ritual gesture for ridding a place of undesirable spirits in a landscape, in places like the Bakongo region in Central Africa (1999:43). Placing African American spirituality in a broader context removes it from the narrow notion of only being coupled with religion, specifically Black Christianity, and expands our thinking to include how captive Africans experienced and practiced in ways far beyond the gaze of the enslaver, overseer or historian.

There are several discussions in historical archaeology about ritual and items that demonstrate the presence of alternative forms of worship among captive peoples. The connections to a general African worldview have long been debated; however, I argue that if we are in conversation with the elements of what these worldviews are, we may move beyond conjecture and begin to bring together theory, conjecture and past practices. We are fully accepting of the notion that African spirituality has continued to influence Black cultural production throughout the diaspora; therefore, it should not be so hard to contemplate the role of animistic spiritual practices in the distant past (Thompson 1983). For example, "For the Yoruba, places where land and trees converge with water are thought to be sites of great spiritual energy, as is any place where two natural forces come together" (Zauditu-Selassie 2009: 100). Nature as a spiritual force, the source of living in balance, is what the in-between is about. In some ways it can be seen as an extension of the Black domestic realm, the homeplace.

Applying Black Feminist Archaeology to the Captive Landscape

During a conversation with my grandmother, I asked about sweeping yards and if she had ever heard of such a thing. She paused and started to smile and replied that she had not thought about sweeping yards in years. Then she replied, "Of course we swept the yard, most people did back then in the country" (Jones, personal communication, 1997). It was an extension of the living space, a part of the house where most of life happened. The house she remembered the most had a separate kitchen, so the yard was literally at the center of the living space, where food was prepared, games played, and people came to visit and socialize. To keep the yard clear of grass and debris, sweeping was just another Saturday chore, overseen by my great-great-grandmother, her grandmother, everyone called "Nine." The sweeping was a chore she really hated to do. So when I started to tell her about my work at the Hermitage and all this research I was doing on yardscapes and the ritual of sweeping yards, she set me straight and told me, "Baby, that was just everyday life, those are everyday things, why are people researching stuff like that?" (Jones, personal communication, 1997). It was a good question, and when I think back to the entire conversation, I often remember how it helped me keep things in perspective and not over "intellectualize" the work I was trying to do. With extreme intellectualization we can remove ourselves from the relevancy of contemporary issues and therefore ways to connect with descendant communities living in the present. It was my grandmother that helped me to see this early in my archaeological career. Although she is no longer living, I still in many ways write with her in mind and laugh at myself when I get a little too starry eyed and hyper-intellectual.

The main reason I had that first conversation with my grandmother is because I had absolutely no real experience with yards. As a second-generation apartment dweller from New York City, activities such as sweeping a yard were outside of my frame of reference. These foreign practices (as in Southern) forced me to take into account the diversity of the African American domestic experience. I began to contemplate the lack of rural experience I had going into plantation archaeology and compared that with the experiences my grandmother must have had coming from rural North Carolina to an urban metropolis like New York City, where she moved in the late 1930s. I contemplated practices and rituals she left behind and thought about the systems of exchange, communication, and everyday experiences that shaped her domestic history in New York. I quickly began to recognize that the captive African household could in no way be confined to the four walls of a twenty by twenty foot dwelling. It had to extend out into the larger environs, including the "yard" (Gundaker 1993, Heath & Bennett 1999).

To understand the lives of captive communities, archaeologists often look at the surface meanings of environment and space. In my analysis, the captive community occupied a bounded and culturally significant space that was not just the background, but epicenter of Black cultural production. Quarter neighborhoods have been referred to by scholars as spaces of autonomy and independence (Blassingame 1972, Davis 1981, Joyner 1984, Franklin 1997a, White 1999, Heath & Bennett 1999, Wilkie 2000, Young 2003, Battle 2004). Similarly, my research had to more fully interpret these protected social spaces of the quarters and complicate yard areas where culture was transformed, cultivated and maintained. This simple yard space was exactly where everyday activities of food preparation, childcare, clothing repair and adornment, recreational storytelling, and music making served as a focal point of captive domestic life and provided venues for strengthening social relationships. Although I argue that there was a shared sense of domestic obligation, these zones of domestic production were still dominated in many ways by captive African women. By concentrating archaeological interpretation on a quarter area I was able to more clearly recognize how landscapes and people come together to tell a story of life, community, and survival.

Homeplace, the Complex Household, and Domestic Exchange

Archaeologists have in several cases investigated historic sites from an anthropological perspective of the household (for examples see Beaudry 1989; Spencer-Wood 1991; Barile & Brandon 2004; Fesler 2004; Franklin 1997a, 2001; Young 2003; Wilkie 2000, 2003). One of the central goals of this work is to communicate with archaeologists ways we can forward our analyses of captive African households by considering the practice of multiple family cooperative domestic exchanges. By identifying the diversity of captive quarter communities we can more holistically understand how these communities shaped and manipulated the built and natural environment to satisfy their own collective needs. Through the development of understanding how a multi-family cooperative domestic exchange system functioned, I can more easily lay out my *complex plantation household model*.

I arrived at a working definition of the captive household after reviewing the literature on the Black family in the past and present. My references were heavily influenced by the work of feminist, particularly Black Feminist, scholars who wrote about the Black family and the role of women in African American social life (Davis 1981, Jones 1985, hooks 1990, White 1999, Wallace 1999, Spillers 2003). However, I needed to understand how captive African families maintained an existence within a normalized, but impossible to emulate, Western patriarchal family structural system. By this I mean that in a social atmosphere where women and children were protected by men as property and dependents, the captive African family operated at a great disadvantage. There was a social expectation of man as head of household; yet realistically, captive African men were usually restricted in their ability to protect, provide and "rule" over their household on any plantation. They were captives, property of another man. Therefore from the beginning, their role as patriarch was virtually impossible to exercise (Davis 1981, White 1999).

The domestic sphere was one of the few places where captive Africans felt the comfort, support and love of family and friends. I am bringing together theories of yardspace, a key concept in African Diaspora archaeology, and "homeplace," a term coined by Black feminist bell hooks. These two ideas have usually been interpreted separately; however, by combining them and calling it *homespace*, I have enhanced how I see the captive domestic sphere at the First Hermitage site. The lives of captive African women and men were structured by racism, sexism, and multiple levels of oppression. As such, the solace of a place called home takes on an added dimension.

It was a place to regroup, to learn strategies of survival, find strength, and create thoughts of resistance. I initially discovered the idea of homeplace through the work of bell hooks (1990). In her chapter, *A Place Called Home*, hooks describes homeplace as the foundation in the making of the Black subject. She states, "Despite the brutal reality of racial apartheid and domination, one's homeplace was the one site where one could freely confront the issue of humanization, where one could resist" (1990:42). When I read this, I thought about how I was viewing the yard area or yardspace at the First Hermitage site and how this idea could demonstrate the complexity of that space in the lives of the First Hermitage Quarter inhabitants. Then I thought about the physical place where one's humanity is restored and began to see the landscape a little differently. I was struck by this metaphor and was reminded of my first reading of Linda Brent's *Incidents in the Life of a Slave Girl*. I was always impressed by her tenacity, her strength to remove herself from slavery, and stay close to protect and see her children from behind the shadows. I compared Linda Brent's description and use of the home of her grandmother as both the source of love, comfort, nurturing, and a place that removed her from slavery to painstakingly regain her humanity (Yellin 1987).

So then one has to understand what *home* means for different people. As I stated earlier, my childhood home was an apartment on the sixteenth floor of a thirty-three story building surrounded by neatly placed trees and play areas, concrete, and parking garages. However, my home was not confined to the many walls of my two-bedroom apartment. It was the playground, the community center, my babysitter's house, my grandmother's apartment on the nineteenth floor of another huge building, the schoolyard, the basketball court, and the *bodega* or "corner store." I began to think about my *homespace* as my environment, the spaces that shaped my experiences and memories. I did not grow up in an individualized place; in many ways there was a collective nature where I grew up. We really had no choice; we were all on top of each other. Different people took interest in what I was doing, where I was doing it and had no problem telling my mother or grandmother when I was not doing right. So, if this was my experience, why is it so difficult to expand the captive household beyond the four walls of a cramped, twenty by twenty foot log or brick cabin?

Understanding the idea of yardscape is a good starting point in the thinking of how captive communities maintained a complex balance between life, work, spiritual and communal efforts. When former captive African women and men remembered their lives in bondage, a common point of discussion for interviewers was how their cabins looked. The yard is often remembered as the site for socializing, playing, performing household chores, raising animals, gardening, and "locations for spiritual and cultural expression" (Heath & Bennett 2000:43).

As architectural historian John Michael Vlach has taught us, captive landscapes are imbued with meaning. Vlach also sees a landscape as not only a visual scene or an environmental setting, but as a cultural construction (1993). Captive inhabitants of plantations may not have had a say in the design, construction, or location of their individual dwellings; however, they did shape how the landscape functioned. The enhanced role of captive women within the domestic sphere most likely meant that it was women who were involved in the most immediate (hands on) shaping of the *homespace*. The absence of men in the initial shaping of the First Hermitage site may have been a direct reflection of how these spaces were constructed. It was not that captive men were not agents on this transforming landscape; they simply may have had much less physical time and therefore less influence on *how* the landscape was initially configured. However, I must stress that simultaneously captive men were essential in the shaping and development of the agricultural landscape. It was the clearing of fields, the building of housing quarters, and the understanding of environmental nuances—the hidden spaces—that were also shaped by captive men. Although they may seem like separate spheres (domestic and field) by contemporary standards, they operated in comparative ways in the daily lives of captive Africans (Battle-Baptiste 2010).

As *homespaces*, these sites become the location of culturally prescribed and understood action, yet the internal power and meaning of these spaces must not be overlooked. In contemporary African America, the yard can be the site of conformity or resistance. For many, the yard and soil around the home is private, protected and in many ways sacred. In contemporary models, even the cultural norms of private and public are defined differently both from racial and class perspectives. For example, the meaning of the front yard and backyard, the use of porches and front steps versus decks and patios can all have divergent meanings across racial and cultural lines.

To expand the understanding of landscape as the site for human action, I employ Victor Turner's *communitas*, described in contemporary terms by anthropologist Jafari Allen as "the liberation of human capacities of cognition, affect, volition, creativity from the normative constraints of social statuses enacting social roles" (2004:1). There are, therefore, various scenes in which *communitas* occurs, including the reshaping of particular places. Allen continues by suggesting that these "ad hoc places...become hallowed by the practices which constitute them as hallowed spaces of connection" (2004:12). Landscapes as spaces of connection are often the insular world of African communities across the African Diaspora (Davis 1981, Bush 1990, Malone 1992, Gasper & Hine 1996, Wilkie 2000, Young 2003, Battle-Baptiste 2010a, Franklin 1997a). For my work on the First Hermitage site, it was clear that these spaces were interpolated as "webs of culture, history, and power," and were maintained through strategic practices that may or may not have appeared as political (Allen 2004).

Included in the function and meaning of household and homespace are the spiritual and cultural needs the collective household fulfilled for captive inhabitants. The connection is more substantial than simply recognizing how captive women and men used exterior spaces to reflect their cultural and physical needs; it is also a method to demonstrate how the presence or absence of material can be interpreted as a way of seeing how *homeplaces* functioned for captive inhabitants. When we describe it as a counter-public space, meaning public to Euroamerican eyes and private for captive peoples, we can begin to better grasp the symbolic and meaningful dimensions of household activities and domestic exchanges as forms of expressive culture.

Pierre Bordieu's theory of *habitus* also assisted me in comprehending how social systems are predisposed to function in particular ways, generated and organized by the practice of creating a conscious need for people within a particular group to understand and master skills needed for survival within any given society (1977). Laurie Wilkie expands on Bourdieu's concept by explaining how his main theory of *habitus* can be applied in a plantation context. She states that "Bourdieu's model explicitly seeks to study the impact of the household setting on the individual, and the archaeological record provides insight into the dialogues that shaped that context" (2000:14). For the plantation archaeologist, *habitus* can be realized "as a cultural propriety and normative order that an individual develops through childhood experiences and through everyday practice or action" (Wilkie 2000). Captive African women and men understood their own cultural environment because of their individual (and by extension, collective) experiences, complicating our simplified notions about the method in which people in the past came to understand their surroundings (Wilkie 2000).

When we start with *habitus*, the archaeologist can then translate how material objects are a part of the "social world of communication, and meaning [that] is intrinsic to communication" with each other (Edwards 1998:248). Ywone Edwards-Ingram also points out that based on the study of the African American past, "archaeologists are finding ... fragments of pots, the outlines of houses, and so forth, representing a past material world that not only provided tools for cooking and shelter, but also served as symbols that reinforced people's views of themselves as culturally distinct from others" (1998: 256).

The communication of ideas and meaning is also directly connected to identity formation. For captive Africans, it was captivity that was the "root of an emergent collective identity" and therefore a collective memory, in which individual experiences differ, but the overall impact on the African Diasporic identity is linked to the collective nature of the social strains created by capture (Eyerman 2001). For it was slavery that "distinguished a race, a people, or a community," depending on the level of abstraction (Eyerman

98

2001:1). It was also slavery that informed the details and rules needed for maintaining the necessary survival tools taught to successive generations. Without these tools, children were subject to learning by mistake instead of example. This "cultural process" and form of trauma is "mediated through various forms of representation and linked to the reformation of collective identity and the reworking of collective memory" (Eyerman 2001:1).

Although much of the communication between captive peoples went unnoticed by enslavers, landscape served as a meaningful aspect of plantation construction. Enslavers were very specific about how they ordered their properties. The placement of a main house, outbuildings, crops, workspaces, and quarter areas was all crafted to maintain order and the display of power (Vlach 1993, Paynter 2000, Epperson 1999). The archaeological analysis of life under slavery and the role of material culture have been generally overlooked in African Diaspora studies. With this book I see a potential to bridge this divide by demonstrating how the understanding of contemporary archaeologists can be a tool for expanding ideas and interpretations of captive life across time and space. The ideologies of captive peoples are actively expressed in landscapes as visual symbols that archaeologists identify and interpret (Massey 1994). The challenge is to "disentangle the various strata that represent physical changes to the land or changing land-use practices to analyze the changing symbolic meanings of the landscape over time" (Yamin & Methany 1996: xv).

In the sense that landscape served as a functional and integral component of the lives of captive communities, these living spaces can be seen as a form of material culture, and thus, as a part of the archaeological record. So, I can then translate the yard *homespace* into a type of artifact. This artifact cannot fit into a lab, but should be incorporated into the overall interpretation of a particular site. In other words, focusing on the relationship between people and landscapes allows the researcher to see the landscape as a text, a source of study that enhances the dialogue of people and their lives. "When time and opportunity presented themselves, sacred symbols and signs became part of who Africans were in the New World. For the most part, their meanings are now faded from traditional history. African American homes and yards abound with African characteristics of expression which still speak to the power and the protection of the ancestors" (Jones 1998:107).

If landscape is the stage for human action, it both reflects past activities and encodes the cultural landscape in which people's views of the world are formed. It is difficult to identify individual families when the dwelling area is limited and there are many "domestic" activities that are conducted communally (Wilk & Netting 1984). In what I see as a complex household, activities are carried out collectively, and the connection between household and yardscape is where all of this action happens. At the First Hermitage site, these collective activities connected multiple families through a system of domestic cooperative exchange, forming a single multi-family household. As follows, the *homespace* (or transformed exterior spaces) functioned as the nucleus of this complex household. The *homespace* was central to the quarter, a significant component to all the members of the quarter neighborhood. The First Hermitage site provided the material and archaeological evidence to address methods employed by captive women and men to form semiautonomous, secure spaces, where various forms of Black cultural production were performed.

Several leading scholars of Black family life have argued against viewing the Black family structure as "pathological" in comparison to the Eurocentric concept of the nuclear family (Stack 1974, Gutman 1976, Davis 1981). However, Black Feminist scholars have long understood how domestic production was directly linked to Black cultural production and the formation of African American identity (Davis 1981, Carby 1987, hooks 1990, Steady 1993, White 1999, Collins 2000, Franklin 2001). My position seeks to challenge interpretations that maintain patriarchy as the norm and to argue that captive women were not relegated to the domestic sphere (Steady 1993). As Davis (1981) explains, the quarters for captive women and men became the single space on the plantation that could facilitate a sense of autonomy or semblance of safety. The *homespace*, therefore, served as the setting where activities of resistance occurred with greater frequency and represents a useful line of evidence to incorporate into a gendered perspective of the captive landscape.

My interpretation of the captive African household seeks to add a new dimension to how daily life differed from Jackson's notion of how the community was structured. As women and men performed household related tasks throughout the plantation, individual families constantly shifted social divisions to meet their varying needs. All members of the quarter were involved in First Hermitage Quarter domestic related activities such as gathering wood, maintaining and cultivating herbs and vegetables, sweeping yards, making soap, mending and repairing clothes, preparing food, or keeping watch over small children and the sick (Battle 2004). These individuals were never listed on inventories according to their domestic occupations, but they were central to the well being of the quarter sub-community. Thus, the enslavers' records do not take into account the layers of cooperative domestic responsibilities performed by captive individuals.

The Archaeology of *Homespace*

Before captivity, African peoples had family and kinship structures that existed in very different ways from the social situations they were thrust into (Gomez 1998). These details of pre-captive life were altered, not completely forgotten, upon arrival in the Americas (Du Bois 1939, Mintz & Price 1992, Gaspar & Hine 1996, Berlin 2000, Sweet 2003, Smallwood 2008). Jackson's classification of simple family "units" of man, woman and children seems the logical place to start when trying to understand the captive community and individual neighborhoods. However, real life did not allow for this to be the norm. To complete daily tasks, captive workers pooled their resources to fulfill the needs of everyone. For the inhabitants of the First Hermitage Quarter, communal living was not simply a cultural choice, but a necessity.

Communication of ideas and meaning is also directly connected to the notion of identity formation. It was also captivity that informed generation after generation the details and rules needed for survival. Without the social space to sit down and communicate, social reproduction of the African American identity would have been nearly impossible. It is not only the physical space for the collective memories of older generations to nurture the succeeding generations; it brings added importance to my theories of yardscapes and *homespaces*.

The captive inhabitants across the Hermitage plantation were responsible for cooking and food preparation. Jackson provided rations of salted pork (upwards of two hundred pigs were slaughtered each year) and other staples based on the number of people in each simple family unit. Owners across the South often complained about how captive laborers were not knowledgable about proper nutrition. John Breedon discusses the general attitude of plantation owners on this subject, "It cannot be expected that the slave who is all day hard at work can pay attention to preparing food after the day's labor. He generally comes home tired, and before he has half cooked his meal, hunger induces him to devour it (Breeden 1980:92). Certain plantations found it impossible to feed large numbers of captive workers on a daily basis. Although some enslavers were involved in how and what captive Africans were preparing to eat, it was in the end a choice of the plantation owner whether to employ a cook to prepare two or three meals per day or leave the chore to the discretion of the workers (Battle 2004). However, even when the plantation owners chose to stay removed from daily food preparation, they were always complaining about the amount of time captive people gave to socializing rather than eating and paying closer attention to maintaining proper health. "The great object is to give them enough, have it well cooked, and *give them time to eat*. Negroes cannot, or will not—they do not—eat in as short time as whites; I can and do eat my meals in from ten to fifteen minutes; they will eat thirty by watch, and ofttimes forty-five; but I have timed them and know it to be a fact" (Breeden 1980:95). This attitude was a marked cultural difference that was of great concern to enslavers, for the regimens of segmented dining dictated that food was to be eaten with proficiency and that the social aspects of dining should take place in gender segregated parlors and other rooms (Shackel 1993).

Figure 2.4: Close up picture of Feature 820, the cooking pit. There was burnt reddish clay at the base of the feature. (Photo by author.)

When I initially came across the idea of plantation owners questioning why captive workers took so long to eat, it was proof-positive that there were clear cultural fissures in even minute aspects of everyday life. It made sense to me, but enslavers could not under-stand that after a long day of work, a person just might want to find a place to sit down and socialize, take time to eat, and relax and take in the benefits of being in a safe place. Then I found one of the most incredible cultural spaces at the First Hermitage site. I call it "the cooking pit," but what it really symbolized was the heart of the First Hermitage *homespace*.

The cooking pit, known as Feature 820, was a food-related area where a variety of faunal remains and cooking utensils were found. This pit addresses the probability of in-ground cooking and adds to the evidence that this area was an active social space, shared by all inhabitants of the Quarter.

When we initially began to excavate we continuously found lay-ers of ash deposits and had no idea if they were related to the nearby Kitchen Quarter or if there were some type of fires made outside the cabins (refer to Figure 2.3). However, as we continued to dig, we finally found the brick-lined cooking pit and several significant artifacts. I interpreted this area as a social space because of the material relating to food preparation, cooking activities, and leisure related items such as clay and ceramic marbles, a harmonica part, several straight pins and buttons, three mouth harps, and fish hooks. This meant that at this location all genders and ages came together to make music, play games, and do other activities like prepare food, make soap, and sew worn clothing. Most important of all was the in-ground cooking that was done at this site. These were all activities that left some archaeological trace, and which not only distinguished this area from any other place excavated on the plantation, but opened up the dialogue about daily life in a central gathering place.

Eating was and still is a social activity for people of African descent. For captive Africans, when work was done, that was the time when their bodies became their own again. "At night, especially in the summertime, after everybody had eaten supper, it was a common thing for us to sit outside. The old folks would get together and talk until bedtime" (Raboteau 1978:220). When the First Hermitage site was exclusively occupied by captive families, the central yardscape (area between the Kitchen Quarter and Farm House, see Figure 2.3) served as what I would term as the "visible" center of the community. Yet, it was the cooking pit (Feature 820) that was the intimate gathering place or central hearth and served as the "hidden" center of life for the occupants (Scott 1990). As stated before, the gathering place (Feature 820) was surrounded by dwellings, which obscured it from Jackson's view and possibly the direct view of the overseer. It was well within the boundaries of the complex Quarter household, and served as the space that tied the various dwellings together; the social heart where multiple families participated in daily functions and activities. So, the observations of enslavers were true, captive people took their time to eat; socializing and tending to the chores of any given day all happened within the same span of time in the same location.

The First Hermitage Quarters did not have obvious boundaries, but the inhabitants were able to manipulate the landscape in a

Figure 2.5: Hannah Jackson, also known as "Old Hannah," and two great-grandchildren at the Hermitage. (Photo courtesy of the Hermitage Museum.)

way that was meaningful for them. The visually and culturally hidden aspects of life under slavery were a daily negotiation of all captive African populations. The ability to construct an outdoor hearth was very real for the members of the First Hermitage community who sat outside on warm nights and shared music, gossip, stories, and good food cooked in ways distinct to the families sharing the social space. Jackson or any overseer might not have found any of these activities threatening or dangerous; they probably appeared as one less obligation for effective plantation management. For the First Hermitage community, however, these actions were the very foundation of their complex household, their *homespace*.

Conclusion

Viewing landscape as the text in which archaeologists must read, it follows that artifacts then become like words on paper. They provide the language through which people express themselves (Shackel 1993). The material realm adds a dimension to the flat, static places that archaeologists interpret. We primarily use ceramics as one of the most efficient ways to analyze historic sites because of the important role they played in the industrial revolution of the eighteenth and nineteenth centuries and because they demonstrate technological innovations and consumption patterns (Majewski & O'Brien 1987, Miller et al. 1994, Thomas 1995, Mullins 1999). However, in my work ceramics mean more than the analysis of consumption patterns and evidence of "hand-me-downs." I see these as symbolic capital that helps to paint a picture of community interaction, hidden aspects of captive life and the larger relevance of material culture analysis.

The development of meaningful extended kin networks and collective labor and knowledge were integral parts of the captive African experience. Using the First Hermitage site as a microcosm of the larger Hermitage captive community, I see archaeological features, material culture associated with specific tasks, and oral and written history all supporting the idea that the lives of captive people can be seen directly in their relationship to their *homespaces* and the larger plantation landscape.

For the captive population, the plantation landscape became the physical space where resistance and autonomy were practiced daily. These spaces existed as contested ground because of the ways the captive community viewed their surroundings. At the Hermitage, Jackson shaped and designed the plantation to reflect self-sufficiency, productivity and order. The quarters were in many ways understood by all plantation inhabitants as the realm of captive people, but this did not mean that they viewed their immediate environment in the same ways as the plantation owner or overseer. With the aid of Black Feminist Archaeology, I explored how archaeological evidence can offer a glimpse into how the captive landscape served as the location of Black cultural production within the plantation context. Through the presence and absence of material at various locations at the First Hermitage site, I see the quarter community as more than a number of families grouped together, but as a complex household that performed everyday duties purposely and collectively.

Landscapes are loaded with symbolism and cultural value, and this was true for captive laborers. Rebecca Yamin and Katherine Methany (1996:xv) describe the relationship between culture and landscapes as "[being] created in terms of human use through action and perception and…loaded with cultural meaning in specific historical contexts." They further argue that since the landscape embodies culture, its symbolism would vary between diverse groups (Yamin & Methany 1996). The enduring legacy in the social memories of contemporary authors and researchers is further evidence of this need to constantly expand our notions of African Diasporic identity and people of African descent living in the past. Viewing memory as symbolic discourse tends to downplay the impact of material (and at times expressive) culture as subjective and emotional in comparison to the traditional emphasis on the textual. Yet, it is upon this memory that so many aspects of African American material and expressive culture rely. These memories become the instruments of knowledge that shape what becomes the social world of people of African descent. Therefore, without the use of alternative resources, many of the intimate details of the African American past remain hidden in the past. This study combines aspects of anthropological and archaeological methodologies to ensure that objects enter into the equation, to give meaning to the overall interpretation of life in captivity. The archaeological analysis of captive African social structures, the physical and spiritual needs of captive laborers, and complex interpretations of space and place at sites such as the Hermitage plantation will enhance the ways we interpret the history of the African Diaspora and its people.

CHAPTER III

Revisiting Excavations at Lucy Foster's Homestead

This chapter is about three women. These women are from different ethnic and racial backgrounds, social and economic classes, divergent life situations, and different time periods. What connects these women is their ability to swim upstream, and go against what is and was expected of them. The first of the three was a freedwoman named Lucy Foster, who lived a long and rewarding life and left behind a very interesting glimpse into the relationship between a person and her material culture. Her story is one of an ordinary woman who would have gone unnoticed if not for the curiosity of an anthropological archaeologist named Adelaide Bullen who excavated her homesite in the 1940s. The second woman, Adelaide Bullen, was a pioneering woman who challenged the social limitations set by a patriarchal academic system and let her own curiosities lead her to tell the story of Lucy Foster. Her tenacity and attention to detail should have forever placed her into the history of African Diaspora archaeology, which I hope from this day forward it does. And finally, the last of the three is me. It is through Lucy and Adelaide that I have learned about myself, my own struggles, and my own desire to make an impact on the world. These two other women have given me inspiration, by what makes us different and what we share. They have helped me to write a book about how race, gender and class can transform the way archaeologists interpret historic sites. It is not just through archaeology that I seek this truth; it is a new kind of archaeology, not afraid to be wrong, debated or discussed; it is a Black feminist archaeology that sees the value of all people and their contributions to our own lives, choices and decisions.

Introduction

Historical archaeologists must develop an approach towards documentary analysis that is uniquely their own. (Deetz 1996:1)

Some readers might protest (at least privately) that few moments have tended to be recorded on the pages of the history of greatness in archaeology because few women were great. This is a dicey and to a certain extent circular issue. If the history is written by people representing or at least operating compliantly within a tradition that validates erasure, how will we expect to judge the possibility of greatness? If we do not even hear of the silenced women, how will we ever be in a position to reckon with them? (Cohen & Joukowsky 2007:8)

When students enter into an undergraduate or graduate historical archaeology class, they learn about the beginnings of the discipline. They often learn the theoretical foundations of the field and the movements among process, culture, and material. They read the canonical texts, by men such as J. C. Harrington, James Deetz, John Cotter, Ivor Noël Hume, Stanley South, and Robert Schuyler to name a few. One thing these sites and works have in common in this category is that the field was established by Euroamerican males. These early sites focused on understanding the lives of other great Euroamericans and then shifted to include other Euroamerican people whose status was beyond the consideration of historical studies. However, although the paradigmatic shift from great men to folks of lesser interest was a progressive one, the field itself was still suffering from racism, sexism and classism in the people who practiced archaeological fieldwork.

I had come to the world of archaeology to find the answers to the questions that history just could not answer. The summer before I started to sit in on these archaeological seminars, I was in the field. We did read, but the articles focused on African American archaeology, African American history and culture. I was thrust into archaeology quickly, and my first field experience was at a plantation site, Rich Neck Plantation in Williamsburg, Virginia, the dissertation site of my soon to be dissertation advisor, Maria Franklin. I really felt that I had been immersed in the field enough that the courses would be exciting and add to my graduate experience. However, the initial entry into archaeological theory and history was strangely Euroamerican and reminded me a great deal of history. I was reading and writing about more Euroamerican men looking at the material of other Euroamerican men (with a few women stirred in) and not really getting a sense of how these graduate seminars and all of this reading was going to conquer or even begin to address the core issues in a larger understanding of race or gender.

I decided to stay; there had to be more; we began to learn about the different branches of post-contact archaeology. I gravitated toward African American archaeology; it was my reason for leaving history. I then began to obsessively read all about the early plantation sites through the work of Charles Fairbanks, John Otto, William Kelso, Theresa Singleton, more James Deetz, Dennis Pogue and Esther White, Paul Shackel and Barbara Little (Pogue & White 1991; Singleton 1995; Orser 1996, 1998b, Fairbanks 1984; Kelso 1986; Deagan 1995; Otto 1984; Shackel 1993; Little 1994b). In conjunction we were learning about gender and feminist approaches to pre- and post-contact archaeology in the Americas (for example, see Beaudry 1989, Gero & Conkey 1991, Brumfiel 1991, Spencer-Wood 1991, Spector 1993, Wall 1994, Wright 1996, Claassen 1997). However, through my training, I only briefly recall any reference to the Lucy Foster site (popularly known as Black Lucy's Garden), and I certainly had not thought twice about the contributions of Ripley or Adelaide Bullen, who first excavated the site in 1942 (Bullen & Bullen 1945). As I increased my archaeological knowledge, I also began to learn about these "obscure" sites that never made it into the general texts and articles assigned in historical archaeology classes. I first heard of Lucy Foster when I read an article by Vernon Baker (1982) in a method and theory class taught by Maria Franklin my first year at the University of Texas. Baker, Euroamerican, wrote about the Foster site with an artifact based analysis. The article piqued my curiosity, but I did not categorize it as a significant African American site at the time. It would not be until I returned to the Northeast to teach at the University of Massachusetts Amherst and was developing the concept for this book that I thought about revisiting this history of the site, this obscure place that was deep in my memory, but hidden by my lack of understanding of the importance of Lucy Foster's existence.

Writing this chapter is intimidating in many ways. I felt a great deal of responsibility about writing about Lucy Foster and her little house in Andover in a way that would reveal who she was as a person. Part of the responsibility lies in telling as much of her story as possible. This chapter could potentially breathe life into her memory, mark the importance of her moment on the planet, and give her experiences and homesite solid footing in the history of the discipline. Her story has the potential to be a cornerstone of how we come to understand the basis of African American, African Diasporan, and post-contact Americanist archaeology. With that in mind, I selfishly want her to be remembered in a respectful and realistic way. I am not here to write her narrative, but to place her site, her material, her life in the historical memory of as many archaeologists as possible. She can bring attention to the hypocrisy of captivity and the lived injustice of the North. A way to look at an everyday person that experienced multiple layers of racism, subtle or otherwise, and add to the larger than life experiences of people such as Frederick Douglass, Harriet Tubman, or Sojourner Truth. Lucy Foster could be any one of our ancestor spirits that hold much larger significance in African American history.

Vernon Baker's article, *Archaeological Visibility of Afro-American Culture: An Example from Black Lucy's Garden, Andover, Massachusetts*, begins with the question of whether Lucy Foster was African or

American born. This was something that seemed interesting at first, but when I began a conversation with Barbara Brown, executive director of the Lawrence History Center in Lawrence, Massachusetts, and Eugene Winter, Honorary Curator at the Robert S. Peabody Museum of Archaeology at Phillips Academy, I began to learn a great deal about the details of Lucy Foster's life. There was clear evidence that Foster was born in America, not Africa. Barbara Brown and Gene Winter had developed a small traveling exhibit about Lucy Foster, Adelaide Bullen and the use of documentary evidence in historical archaeology.

Baker's work was to properly place the Foster homesite into the larger field of African American archaeology. His 1978 report brought the Bullens' work up to date with current trends in the ceramic data analysis of the time. I was always struck by the material focus of the report, however Baker's work was simply following the philosophy that ceramics were dateable and reflected "aspects of the behavior of those who acquired and used them" (Baker 1978: 2). Ceramic analysis centers on many factors. Dating ceramics is important to understanding accessibility to markets, importation patterns, personal and cultural tastes, and how style and decoration are reflective of the people who owned them (Baker 1978).

> Thus, while the archaeologist owes a debt to and relies heavily upon the work of the ceramic historian, it is essential also to study ceramic items from beneath the ground. Only by augmenting "collectable" pieces with archaeological items from primary, cultural contexts can a more complete picture of the range of ceramics once in use be achieved. Even though it may never be possible to assign the many varieties of edge-decorated pearlware plates to particular potters, descriptions of the many motifs may contribute to an understanding of what was produced, sold, used, and discarded. By noting associations among the shapes and decorative motifs of ceramic items, the type of site, its geographical location, and the occupation and social and economic position of its occupants, we may provide further information about the interpretive value of such items. (Baker 1978: 2)

Baker's main goals were to establish "Black Lucy's Garden" as an important site of study for a detailed analysis of ceramics on a nineteenth century New England site, and to further the site as an example of how the ceramic vessels found at the site "reflect Afro-American culture" (Baker 1978: 2). In the quest to understand the African American past, there has been a historical overemphasis on slavery that in many ways has created "the illusion that the balanced conveying of experiences within the diaspora is instead a romantic need to reconceptualize a history of slavery and disempowerment" (Leone et al. 2005: 577). With this as my foundation, I began my quest to find out who Lucy Foster really was, and demonstrate how Black Feminist Archaeology will help in this mission.

Past Interpretations of Lucy Foster's Homestead

Baker's article is written at a time when one of the main focuses in African American archaeology was to recognize distinct "slave consumption patterns," and to try to make sense of ratios of bowls to flatware or plates and how this translated to cultural choice. There is a clear distinction being made about how these different populations would "look" materially (Otto 1977). So, it was no surprise that Baker was looking for how Lucy Foster's ceramic assemblage would resemble the material pattern of a plantation site, even though she was a freed African woman living in Eastern Massachusetts (Baker 1978:34). Another aspect of pattern recognition from this time period was to look for a symbolic pattern in food consumption. It appears that people of African descent, whether captive or freed, were not known to have consumed butchered bones with the same frequency as Euroamericans (they chose chopped bones rather than sawed). In his work on Cannon's Point Plantation, John Otto demonstrated a correlation between social status, shapes of ceramics and dietary habits (Otto 1977). Baker concludes, "In terms of faunal remains, 82 percent of the cattle, sheep, and hog remains is chopped and cleaved open, suggesting that stews, not roasts, are the main bill of fare" (1978:111). This reasoning seems simplistic and in some ways even essentializing by today's standards; however, when Baker is engaging in this work, this was seen as cutting edge and innovative. I do want to stress that his reanalysis of the ceramic assemblage is a very positive move for the site's overall visibility within the field.

The next layer of interpretation in African American patterns was the construction of Lucy's house. For Baker, he wanted to test if Lucy's house was a reflection of a classic African American architectural pattern (see for examples of African American architecture Vlach 1990, 1993). Baker states,

> The twelve-foot dimension, as Deetz notes,...assumes great significance in light of John Vlach's recent research on shotgun houses in the American South and in Haiti, and on West African house types. Vlach...has identified the shotgun house as a legitimate Afro-American architectural form. This is especially important since architectural units at Parting Ways strongly resemble shotgun houses in both floor plan and dimension. The twelve-foot module, then, may represent a distinctive Afro-American architectural tradition. (1978: 112)

Baker also felt that the construction of Lucy's house was probably influenced by her tastes and the amount she had to spend (1978: 35). Although the architectural footprint of Lucy's house was approximately square, Baker asserts that it did fit the twelve-foot pattern. I still think this is rather confusing, but according to Baker, this house appears to be evidence of a cultural choice on Lucy's part.

Baker comes to some interesting conclusions toward the end of his interpretation of the site; the most intriguing is if the patterns discovered can be seen as a reflection of being a site occupied by an African American or a site occupied by a poor person. Baker then begs the question, "The issue, then, is that the patterns visible in the archaeological record may be reflecting poverty and not the presence of Afro-Americans" (1978:113). Often, according to John Otto, the assemblages of overseers would be similar (especially for faunal remains) to those of captive Africans in plantation contexts (Otto 1977). Therefore, which becomes the main focus of interpretation, poverty or race? Do they become the same?

Whether in the 1940s or the 1970s, the questions about people of African descent often circulate around difference and cultural choices that are divergent from Euroamerican norms and practices. The open ended conclusions by archaeologists such as Baker speak volumes about the attitude toward Black and white women and work outside of the safety of patriarchal controlled domestic spaces. Lucy Foster's site provides a glimpse into a distinct site occupied by a woman who had to work inside and outside of her home to survive. What role that played in the way that the Bullens and Baker understood the site may never be known, however. This is why it remains essential for us to look back, reflect, and at times even alter sites that were excavated and interpreted in the past. How was the site thought of in the 1940s by the Bullens, in the 1970s and 1980s by Vernon Baker, and now by myself in 2011? The conclusions will be based on varying circumstances, changes in theoretical methodologies, and ultimately, the subject position of the archaeologist engaging in the newest interpretive process.

Another question is, how were the analyses of three Euroamerican archaeologists influenced by their relationship (or lack thereof) with the African descendant community? Would this information even make it beyond a local Archaeological Society bulletin or a field report sponsored by an archaeology museum in Eastern Massachusetts? Is her story used in any way to tell the story of a woman of African descent from New England? Her life on paper, her appearance on the Andover dole, all give indications that she was among the poor. This paper trail if understood by itself would only point to her needing assistance; however, I want to argue that by adding the other factors of her documentary footprint, it is not so clear. Lucy Foster was most likely dependent on income from domestic service and associated forms of manual labor. Her income therefore would have been sporadic and limited in many ways. This I am sure was a factor in her overall lifestyle and would mean she needed help from time to time, as it seems in the documentary record (see table 3.1).

The sheer volume of her ceramic assemblage begs the question of what does the "pattern" analysis model used by Baker say about

116

Year	Amount of Dole
1813–1821	$1.00 per year
1822–1823	1.50 per year
1824–1825	2.00 per year
1826	3.00
1827	1.50
1828	2.00
1829	No records
1830–1835	2.50 per year
1836	3.00
1837–1838	5.00 per year
1839–1845	4.00 per year

Table 3.1: Lucy Foster's Annual Dole from the Fund for Relief of Indigent Persons in the South Parish Congregational Church, Andover, Massachusetts. (Based on Baker 1978:7.)

market access, hand-me-downs, and limited gross income. Was poverty the same in Andover in the 1820s as it was in the 1840s, when she was much older and getting sick? How does one maintain the status of being constantly poor; is it defined externally or is it self-induced? I am confident that attitudes about this site have changed over time, but I must keep in mind that historical archaeology has a history of misunderstanding of the ways "race" is lived and experienced, gender is acknowledged, and ultimately for me, how race, gender and class overlap, intersect and contradict each other all at once (Franklin 1997c, Patten 1997, Orser 1998b).

In the mid-1940s intensive archaeological excavations at the site of an African American woman born into slavery look very different from today. The interpretation would probably been shaded a little with unfamiliarity of Black life in New England, no larger dialogue about the material culture of race or gender, and a very distinctive approach to artifact recovery and analysis. Ripley and Adelaide were investigating an Indigenous site when they "stumbled" across the foundations of the Foster homesite (Brown, personal communication, 2010). In the 1940s it was becoming more and more difficult to travel outside of the United States as a result of World War II (Winter, personal communication, 2010). I believe that Ripley was intrigued by digging a house foundation and the preservation of the site; it was something most archaeologists could not resist. For Adelaide, I think there was excitement with the site. However, I think it was also the opportunity to learn about and find the story of the freedwoman who lived there, almost irresistible for a female anthropologist. The material was not only aesthetically pleasing, but its association with the site and the story meant that the story of Lucy Foster would forever be a part of Massachusetts history, at least for brief moments in time.

This is a story of race and gender. This is a story of women's lives and their histories. This may also be an interesting look into the relationship between Black and White women from the vantage point of a New England town where freedom was in many ways taken for granted. With captivity a thing of the recent past and a place where larger plantations were not the norm, newly freed women and men in a place like Massachusetts experienced a unique transitional movement from captivity to freedom.

Telling the story of Lucy Foster is important in a variety of ways. Her story addresses the invisibility of Black women, their daily lives, their labor, and their overall presence. How does a legal precedent stop the foundation of race and racism from affecting the lives of Black people (even in the category of free)? So much energy and/or emphasis is placed on the emancipation of captive Africans that we then move away from a critical analysis of what life meant for free people of color in Northeastern states like Massachusetts. They become the taken for granted details of life that I hope can be part of the archaeological interpretation of a site such as Lucy Foster's acre. This site holds a key to a deeper understanding of the aftertaste of slavery in the lives of these freed people.

Adelaide Bullen and Black Lucy's Garden

The two issues—women doing archaeology and looking for gender in the past—are inseparable because one's gender (the cultural role only loosely based on biological sex) is a major part of the enculturation process and cannot help but influence how one does science, whether in choice of issues to investigate or interpretation of results. (White 1999:6)

One of the earliest examples of historical archaeology in the United States and excavation of the site of an Afro-American is Adelaide and Ripley Bullen's excellent research conducted in 1943 at Black Lucy's Garden. (Baker 1978:1)

Archaeology was traditionally the domain of Euroamerican men. Men of means who had the leisure and time to travel to new and exciting places, able to take large blocks of time and uncover and collect pieces of the world's treasures. It was a field about adventure and intrigue, intellectual prowess, and the search for the ultimate material remnant from the past that could tell the most compelling story. These factors did not leave much time for raising children, gardening, reading Victorian novels, hosting tea parties, maintaining a household, or doing a load of laundry. So, the idea of women in archaeology in an age where society still treasured the remnants of Victorian sensibilities and expectations was above and beyond belief.

The stereotypes of gender in the early days of Americanist archaeology seem a bit humorous at first glance, but if you have any experience in the lab or field, you may have come across such ideas.

It could be argued that the way women are traditionally socialized in our society makes them well suited for field and lab management, with better skills in scheduling, health and safety, and attention to tiny details of forms, tables, microflakes, or palynology [the study of pollen grains or other spores]...Other studies have noted the female tendency to prefer/excel in perceived tedious tasks such as sorting lithic debitage, while males prefer analysis of big things thought to be more important, such as whole points, or concentration of their efforts upon field-work. (White 1999: 14)

To direct fieldwork, one needs to be trained to do this job. Often, women were disadvantaged in the training because they could not find sites that allowed their participation (White 1999). It was the Workers Progress Administration that was probably the most vanguard when it came to complicating gendered divisions of site management (see the discussion of the Irene Mound site in the introduction to this book). Field experiences meant more than excavation; there were real challenges to be overcome in order for women to become a real part of archaeological fieldwork. There were bathroom issues, safety from harassment, issues of managing crews, and being taken seriously in a variety of capacities (Claassen 1999). So, in a small town in Eastern Massachusetts, Ripley and his wife Adelaide discovered an unremarkable house foundation while searching for local Indigenous sites.

This sets the scene for a Euroamerican woman, Mrs. Adelaide Bullen, born in Worcester, Massachusetts, in 1908. She married Ripley Pierce Bullen on July 25, 1929, at the age of twenty-one (Marrinan 1999:149). Ripley Bullen, born in 1902, had already received a degree in mechanical engineering from Cornell in 1925 and was working for General Electric in engineering research. Although he was an engineer by training, he always maintained a serious interest in doing archaeology (Marrinan 1999:149). In 1939, Ripley became a founding member of the Massachusetts Archaeological Society and decided to leave General Electric to accept a position with the Robert S. Peabody Foundation for Archaeology at Phillips Academy in Andover, Massachusetts (Merrinan 1999:149). While Ripley was pursuing a graduate degree from Harvard in Anthropology, Adelaide began an undergraduate degree at Radcliffe. While study-ing at Harvard and Radcliffe, the couple traveled to Chaco Canyon in Arizona to participate in a one week excavation, which yielded three papers, one of which was Adelaide's comparative linguistic research

Figure 3.1: Plan of Lucy Foster Homestead. (From Adelaide Bullen and Ripley P. Bullen, Jan. 1945, Vol. 6, No. 2. Bulletin of the Massachusetts Archaeological Society.)

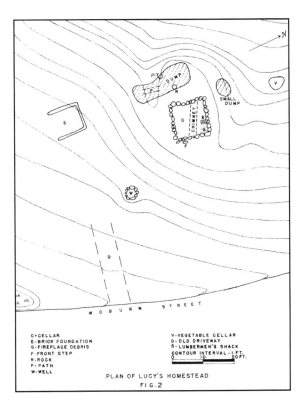

on the occurrences of stuttering among Navajo youth (Marrinan 1999:150). After receiving her A.B. degree from Radcliffe in 1943, at thirty-five, she continued her graduate studies in cultural and physical anthropology also at Harvard (Marrinan 1999:150). In 1943 the Bullens excavated "Black Lucy's Garden" in Andover, Massachusetts, a site that would be one of the earliest studies of "a domestic site related to slavery and the circumstances of free persons of color" (Merrinan 1999:150).

Adelaide was very busy with her family, her studies and advocating for better data on women in physical and cultural anthropology. She was also involved in civilian consulting for the Department of the Army and was a member of the Fatigue Laboratory at Harvard University (Merrinan 2001:151). Her role in the interpretation of the Foster site was invaluable. She went beyond finding historical research on a particular site; she looked for the story of a single freed-woman and opened up a dialogue about her life and, ultimately, what could be considered a forerunner to African American archaeology in the Northeast.

In 1948 Adelaide and Ripley Bullen moved to Gainesville, Florida, for Ripley to accept a position as assistant archaeologist with the Florida Board of Parks and Memorials. In 1952, the Board disbanded and all the data and collections were sent to the Florida State Museum. Ripley moved to the museum and became the first curator of social sciences and served as department chair for seventeen years. Adelaide was involved with the museum by 1949, but was never given a paid position. Her work was on a voluntary basis. Here as before the Bullens worked together to publish several articles and reports of local archaeological sites. However, the couple continued to be seen as outsiders. Their New England roots and family wealth made them "an attractive pair, and many of their initial projects were the result of contacts with wealthy landowners," which was becoming a thing of the past for the field (Merrinan 1999:153). Much of Ripley's work was oversighted by the new generation of archaeologists working in the state (Bluestain, personal communication, 2010). These men had formed strong bonds as male field supervisors and postwar colleagues that in turn changed the class complexion of the archaeological leaders across academic departments throughout the region (Merrinan 1999:153). After Ripley's death, Adelaide struggled to publish her husband's work and struggled even harder to stay in the field she had worked in for decades. Even as time passed, the amazing work she did over her lifetime remains in the shadows of historical archaeology and physical anthropology.

Adelaide's work on Lucy Foster's Acre in my mind marks an important moment in her career, and with this book and chapter I hope to highlight her contribution to the field, for it was her work that brought Lucy Foster to my consciousness. It is because of Adelaide's archival work that anything is known about this one woman born into captivity in the little town of Andover, Massachusetts.

Year	Event	Age
1767	Lucy is born in Boston	0
1771	Taken in by Fosters and is baptized	4
1782	Job Foster dies	15
1783	Slavery ends in Massachusetts	16
1789	Hannah marries Phenious Chandler	22
1791	Lucy is "warned" out of Andover	24
1793	Profession of Faith/Lucy returns to Andover	26
1793	Baptizes her son Peter	26
1812	Hannah Chandler dies	45
1815	Lucy's house is completed	48
1845	Lucy dies of asthma	78

Table 3.2: Lucy Foster's Chronology.

The Story of Lucy Foster, 1767–1845

Lucy Foster was born in 1767 in the city of Boston. This was deduced by church records clearly stating her death on November 1, 1845, when she was 78 years old (South Parish Congregational Church [SPCC] records, Andover, Massachusetts). She first appears in the written record in 1771, when she entered into the Foster household at the age of four. "On July 14, 1771, Sarah, a child given to Job Foster, & Lucy, a Negro child was baptized" (SPCC records). Sarah Gilbert, the other child mentioned, was a young girl taken in by the Fosters to become a part of the working household. Gilbert is listed under "Records of Information of Persons Taking into Town - Service of the Lord. Act of Court in Regard of the Maintenance of poor" (SPCC records). The entry reads, "May 2nd, Sarah Gilbert was taken into town by Job Foster. She came loft from Sewsbury" (SPCC 1771). This was a common arrangement where families would take in children of the poor to provide them with a home, receive compensation from the parish and gain an extra hand in daily household tasks and labor. When trying to reconstruct the Foster household in the early years, there were no Africans or other servants listed in the household before the 1771 tax record. Job and Hannah Ford Foster were married on March 27, 1760 (SPCC, 1760). The couple had their first child, Joseph in 1762 (SPCC, 1762). An interesting detail is that these two young women entered the household eleven years after the marriage of Job and Hannah and were very young. They would have also been children when they first were taken in. The Bullens and Baker both read the primary documents as stating that Lucy and Job Foster received and baptized a girl named Sarah, and therefore interpreted this as proof that Job fathered a child by Lucy, which would have been impossible, for Lucy was only 4 years old in 1771. This small detail may seem insignificant, but has always been a point of contention for me in Lucy's life story. There has been so little written about Lucy Foster that I always wanted to learn more about her circumstances beyond the common assumption of miscegenation as one of her defining qualities.

Lucy Foster's life was a very complex and full one. She served in the Foster household with no written record of any other significant activity or changes. From the age of 4 years old to 15, she served in this household as the only African. There are no further details about Sarah Gilbert, how her life was or how long she stayed in the household. A few years later, in August of 1775, Job and Hannah had a daughter named Mary (SPCC, 1775). So, it is assumed that the household was made up of two adults and four children. Job Foster died of smallpox on January 1, 1782 (SPCC, 1782). Also, within the same year as Foster's death, the historic court cases of Elizabeth Freeman (Mum Bett) and Quak Walker were taking place and beginning the elimination of slavery in Massachusetts. Lucy appears to have stayed on with Hannah Foster after her freedom. I have often wondered how it must have felt to know that the law had declared you a free person, but your choices of employment and movement were limited in many other ways, so service and safety may have made the decision for many newly freed captives in the Massachusetts (Litwack 1965, Paynter 1990, Horton 1993, Melish 1998, Lemire 2009).

Hannah Foster remarries Philemon Chandler, one of the assessors of her late husband's estate, in 1789, when Lucy Foster was 22 years old. Lucy was living with Hannah and her new husband, until a document appears dated February 1791 "warning" Lucy out of town. The document reads, "You are, in the Name of the Commonwealth of Massachusetts, directed to warn and give Notice unto Lucy a Negroe Woman formerly a Servant of Job Foster…" (SPCC, 1791). This practice was not uncommon all over New England cities and towns. They have been interpreted as attempts to reduce the presence of "transient" Black and Indigenous people in towns across New England (Melish 1998). Although much of the rhetoric around emigration back to Africa solidified after 1800, with this establishment of the American Colonization Society in 1816, efforts to discourage large communities of people of color in New England were being practiced by laws such as "warning out" (Melish 1998:165). There was a range of reasons for a person to be "warned out" of town. Among them were things such as eliminating impoverished or undesirable strangers; people not qualified for "legal settlement" in town; people who might be unable to generate rents or other income of a certain value; and people who had accrued charges of "disorderly behavior" or might be "likely to become chargable" (Melish 1998:191). Therefore, the idea that this was a legal means to ensure a productive and upstanding population of any given town is not what is really going on. According to Joan Melish, her analysis of "warning out" in Providence, Rhode Island, concluded that people of color that were being "warned out" were not transients passing through; they had on average lived in Providence for between five and ten years.

This seems like a very significant turn of events for a 24 year old woman to be abruptly removed from the town she has lived in since she was a small child. Two years passed in the Chandler household without incident. It is very hard to imagine what happened to warrant such a strong statement by the town of Andover; however, two years later, Lucy Foster appears to have returned to Andover and is once again recorded in the South Parish Congregational Church records on September 22, 1793. There may have also been a chance that she never left Andover. However, at the age of 26, she is recorded as giving a "Profession of Faith" to the South Parish Congregational Church (SPCC, 1793). Then, one month later, on October 20, 1793, Peter, son of Lucy Foster a Negro Woman, is baptized (SPCC, 1793). There is no indication of how old Peter is, where he was born, or his paternity. Initially, my thoughts were very troubled; it seemed that it took a great effort by local historians and archaeologists like Barbara Brown and Gene Winter to carefully read documents and piece together the life of Lucy Foster and highlight the fact that she did not mother a child by her master Job Foster, then to delve deeper and wonder if there may have been an incident later in her life at the Chandler household that lead to her being "warned out" of town. However, this may, of course, not be the only scenario. She may have left town, met someone and returned to the Chandler household with her son Peter, professing her faith and making sure he was baptized, but it is curious.

Shortly after Lucy reappears in the church records, Philemon Chandler dies, in 1798. Within a few years Hannah is living back on the Foster property in the house of Job, her first husband. It is not clear whether Lucy stays with Hannah full time or whether she may have been living somewhere else, yet she is connected to Hannah in some way. For when Hannah Foster Chandler dies in 1812, her will clearly states:

> I give and bequeath to Lucy Foster, the black girl, who lives with me for heirs, executors and administrators, one cow. I also give devise and bequeath to the said Lucy one acre of land, situated on the left side of the road leading from my house in Andover, and bounded by a line beginning at a pair of ? in the ? next beyond the apple tree...to have and to hold the same to the said Lucy for her natural life. (Hannah Ford Foster Chandler's Last Will and Testament)

Another interesting detail is that in Hannah's will, after her declarative statement, "I, Hannah Chandler...," the first item in the will is what she leaves Lucy. This information appears before she dictates what she leaves her children Joseph and Mary. For me this speaks volumes about the perceived relationship between Hannah and Lucy. Was it all about her appreciation for all the great service Lucy had provided, or was it compensation for never really paying Lucy a decent wage during her lifetime? Is it to make up for a bad situation that happened years before when Lucy was forced out of town? These are questions that I may never know the answer to, but I do not take for granted that it was out of pure kindness and love that Hannah Foster Chandler left Lucy Foster one acre of land, one cow and the sum of $100.00 (SPCC, 1812). This inheritance was significant for many reasons. When Hannah Foster Chandler passed away she had many debts (Brown, personal communication, 2010). After her estate was settled she had no assets left; however, the town of Andover collected the money, gave Lucy the acre she was promised and found a cow. Andover was settled in 1646 and was caught up in most things New England, such as the witchcraft hysteria of the Salem Witchcraft trials, the Northern Anti-Slavery Movement, and the Underground Railroad (Siebert 1936). Andover's unique character was probably one of the reasons that they had a commitment to taking care of "their own." And it appears that Lucy Foster was no exception. In a town as small as Andover, Lucy may have had a place of social prominence that might not be reflected in the analysis of her broken plates and glasses. However, the details of her life open up a story that is both intriguing and inspiring on many levels.

I began to wonder who Lucy Foster was after 1812? The gaps in her life documentation are for me the most intriguing. For example, I questioned where was Lucy between 1791 and 1793, when she was "warned out" of town? Did she leave Andover or did she simply leave Chandler's employ? The there is the other short span of time between 1812 and 1815, after the death of Hannah Foster Chandler and the construction of her new house? In 1812, she was 45 years old and it appears still in good health. She probably, like many freed

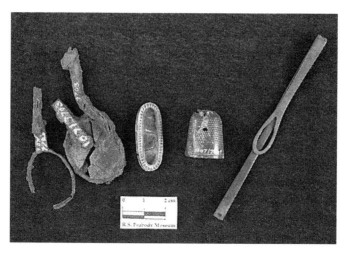

Figure 3.2: Items from the Lucy Foster Homesite.
Eyeglasses, jeweled broach, thimble, and an unknown object.
(Photo courtesy of the Robert S. Peabody Museum of
Archaeology, Phillips Academy, Andover, Massachusetts.)

African women, continued to work in a variety of service jobs, such
as sewing, taking in laundry, keeping house, raising young children, cooking or other domestic duties at places such as the Ballard
Tavern, very close to her house (Brown, personal communication,
2010). Her material assemblage indicates her performing some of
these tasks. For example, sewing; the Bullens found a large number
of buttons, needles, thimbles, scissors, and other equipment relating to sewing and mending.

A point of contention in this reanalysis is the idea that Lucy
Foster was impoverished. This was a central point in the interpretations of Adelaide and Ripley Bullen and Vernon Baker. Baker states,
"Lucy's indigence is demonstrated by the dole she received from the
South Parish Church. Immediately after Hannah's death, Lucy
is identified as needy, and remains one of the parish poor until her
death" (1978: 5). She is listed on the Overseers of the Poor beginning in 1813 until her death; however, she is never asked to leave
her house and relocate to an alms house (which becomes common

Figure 3.3: One of several transfer printed pearlware teacups. (Photo courtesy of Robert Peabody Museum of Archaeology, Phillips Academy, Andover, Massachusetts.)

practice around this time; it had proved to be much more cost effective than to distribute monies across the town). She is listed on the Annual Dole as "Female, aged 66, Colored, born in Boston, unmarried, able to read and write, temperate and living at home [listed as Abroad]." The reason for my discomfort has several dimensions, in my rethinking through the Lucy Foster site, I see her as listed on the Annual Dole record, but my question is how is poverty defined by the Bullens and Baker? Materially, Lucy Foster's assemblage has an incredible variety of items: pearlware, redware, creamware, Chinese porcelain, delftware, jackfield ware, local stoneware and whiteware (Baker 1978: 19). The forms included plates, bowls, cups, saucers, mugs, pitchers, teapots, pans, pots, and jugs, totaling 113 separate vessels (Baker 1978: 109).

So the pressing question is, what does poverty look like in the material record? How is poverty perceived by the archaeologist excavating the site? Could there be a preconceived notion of what types of people are more susceptible to poverty? And lastly, how does poverty shape your identity or how is your identity shaped by poverty? This line of inquiry has always been a constant in my thought process when I interpret sites or read of others' interpretations. I consciously wonder about the invisible connection between race and poverty. In my intellectual training, I do not recall reading an abundance of material about people of African descent who were not poor. Does this influence the way that archaeologists approach an African American site? Do we really need to have a one-to-one correlation comparing an impoverished white homestead to place a freed Black homestead in the proper class trajectory? The material found at Lucy Foster's homesite implores us to think further and question everything that has been a part of the larger interpretive work previously. As I read and reread the work of the Bullens and Baker, I keep seeing a slightly different story. I envision a woman living independently (with help from time to time), well respected, working within a system that gave her freedom, but maintained a level of restriction that she had to maneuver throughout her adult life. I see her as a woman with great wisdom, with a sense of place and time, a woman that was not in isolation, but always had people in her house to talk and share and laugh. I know she was a part (if not one of the central figures) in the small, but tight knit Black community of Andover and North Andover.

There is also the possibility that the assemblage found at Foster's homesite is an indication of her position in the larger Andover community. Her home was on the main road from Boston proper, and her virtual isolation may have been an advantage for night travelers. In the work of Cheryl LaRoche, she "expands our understanding of the Underground Rail Road by introducing free black communities and their associated black churches…as sites of resistance in the American North" (Leone et al. 2005: 579). LaRoche also shows that free black communities "were situated on the landscape, often alongside and overshadowed by more famous abolitionist strongholds" (Leone et al. 2005: 579). It is very possible that her role in the antislavery movement went undocumented and even unnoticed. There was no need for recognition on her part, just the ability to be there as a conduit toward freedom.

Lucy Foster was an ordinary woman with a remarkable story. Dissimilar to people like Elizabeth Freeman (as a captive woman known as Mum Bett), she may have continued on a path of obscurity if not for the discovery of a vegetable cellar hole that had once been a part of her homesite. As I researched Foster's life, I began to learn about incredible women like Elizabeth Freeman and her struggles as a captive African woman in New England. Elizabeth Freeman, the African woman who sued for freedom and won, shared a story of cruelty and sadness that was not so rare for people of African descent in Massachusetts. At a time when captivity was solidified and began to spread to points further west, others were taking their chances and escaping the chains of plantations and urban centers across the South. It was in this climate that Elizabeth Freeman found a way to legally argue that slavery was against the Massachusetts Constitution and morally wrong.

What this Site Means for the Future

> From a theoretical standpoint, P. R. Bullen's research was one of the 'first attempts to devise cultural chronology and hypothesis about the late eighteenth and early nineteenth century American social system from the study of pottery' (Baker 1978). Baker's subsequent analysis of the site tested Otto's ceramic theories. At the time of the original excavation in 1945 and Vernon's reanalysis in 1978, a gendered analysis was not highlighted among historical archaeologists. It is a little surprising, however, that Black Lucy's Garden has not been reanalyzed from a feminist perspective. (Leone et al. 2005: 586)

This site was one of the first African American archaeological sites excavated in the United States. Yet Lucy Foster's Homesite is not a part of our archaeological historical memory. The Lucy Foster site is not taught as a foundational place to students of historical or Americanist archaeology, and her story is certainly not taught to school children in Massachusetts or the larger New England region. Her story is both typical and atypical; it could provide a glimpse of the combining of race and gender at a single site in Massachusetts, but also provide a narrative of a woman who lived at a unique time and place, the end of captivity in a region where slavery was buttressed against growing industry and the large influx of newly arriving European immigrants. This would have been a moment when women and men of African descent were navigating through uncertain terrain. The abolishment of slavery in Massachusetts was not based on a widely held moral compulsion, but on a clever understanding and manipulating of a newly drafted state constitution (Piper & Levinson 2010). The irony is that most likely the crafters of this document rewrote the document to secure the rights and liberty of the state's free Euroamerican citizenry, people that mattered in the eyes of colonial justice. Imagine using a document that was meant to maintain freedom and justice for the free citizens and transforming it into a document to liberate members of society that had yet to be granted citizenship. This is what the court cases of Quak Walker and Elizabeth Freeman (Mum Bett) started; this decision had to have influenced the life of Lucy Foster.

When creating a historical profile of Lucy Foster, I thought about the meaning of freedom for an older freedwoman living on her own in Eastern Massachusetts in the early nineteenth century. I thought about where she lived, the limited and at times isolated African American community surrounding her, her rich ceramic assemblage, her resourceful sources of income, the physical location of her house (on the main road), and her importance in the larger (African descendant and Euroamerican) Andover community. Pulling all these factors together kept me up some nights. There was so much I wanted to see and know about Lucy Foster that writing a chapter on her will, in my opinion, never be complete. I know her story is beyond her position in life or the ceramic assemblage associated with her house.

Lucy Foster, born into captivity, was able to experience freedom for many years, but her daily struggles to survive and live out her life in peace were probably not easy, even living in a place like Andover. I would like to think that despite this, she lent her assistance to those in need and in search of freedom. She is just as important as any famous abolitionist or a woman who sued and won her freedom. For me, this site becomes one of the main foundational sites for a Black Feminist Archaeology. The ability to use a new theoretical approach such as Black Feminist Archaeology to rethink the interpretation of her homestead is a powerful moment of recognition that I hope Lucy would be proud of. Her life, her story, and her house have shaped and moved the theory beyond ideas into a way to create a healing story of struggle and triumph.

CHAPTER IV

The Burghardt Women and the
W. E. B. Du Bois Boyhood Homesite

On my first trip to the W. E. B. Du Bois Boyhood Homesite in Great Barrington, Massachusetts, I had no idea what to expect. I knew there was no standing structure on the property. I knew the site was located directly off a busy and dangerous road, and it was overgrown and teeming with poison ivy. However, my excitement and anticipation kept me open to all the possibilities of what this place looked like. While in graduate school at the University of Texas, one of my mentors was an incredible scholar named Ted Gordon. When I was interviewing for a tenure track job at UMass Amherst, Ted was excited and pushed me to understand the significance of this position. His father (some forty years earlier) was one of the men who purchased the property to create a Du Bois memorial park. UMass became the steward of the property, and our library (named after W. E. B. Du Bois) holds the largest collection of his papers in the world. The idea of having the opportunity to do archaeology at a site associated with Du Bois was a monumental moment in my life. So, here I was standing on the property where this man, this incredible man, ran and played as a boy, and I am here just over a century later, thinking about what a Du Boisian archaeology looks like. As I stepped on the place where the Black Burghardts lived, I felt overwhelmed and anxious. Initially, I got a sense of neglect and sadness. I wanted this place to be so much and didn't quite know how to process what was before my eyes. I listened intently to the history of what had been done at the site— the dedication in 1969, getting National Landmark Status—and things became clearer for me. I began to envision how the site looked at different times in its long and complicated history. I was curious about how this site looked when there was still some physical evidence of a structure, a hearth, a cellar. I wondered what Du Bois looked at, where he might have played and where he might have stood as an adult longing to own the property himself. As Ted once told me, I was destined to be at this place, to do this work, and to get to know Du Bois as a human being. Bob Paynter, who encouraged me to apply for a position at UMass, has become my mentor, colleague and friend. He has been involved with the site for more than twenty years. When I realized that we would figure this place out together, I was humbled and honored at the prospect. I thought about all this on that first visit and once again felt the sacredness that I originally carried with me before I arrived at the site. I sometimes lose myself in thinking of what the future might hold for this, bringing the story to the world in a way that only Bob and I can. The author of great works, one of the founding members of the Niagara Movement, the National Association for the Advancement of Colored People (NAACP), editor of the Crisis Newspaper, and hero of the Pan Africanist movement. He has touched my life at so many different times. His moving to Ghana was one of the main reasons my mom traveled to Ghana immediately after graduating from college; my mentor Ted Gordon's father purchasing the property; and now the first archaeology project beyond my dissertation. Du Bois is now in my system for good. So, as I believe in the power of the past, the importance of ancestors and the significance of place, I want to bring Du Bois back home, forever.

Du Bois's Great Barrington

I was born by a golden river and in the shadow of the two great hills, five years after the Emancipation Participation, which began the freeing of American Negro slaves. The valley was wreathed in grass and trees and crowned to the eastward by the huge bulk of East Mountain, with crag and cave and dark forest. Westward the hill was gentler, rolling up to gorgeous sunsets and cloud-swept storms. The town of Great Barrington, which lay between these mountains in Berkshire County, Western Massachusetts, had a broad Main Street, lined with maples and elms, with white picket fences before the homes. The climate was to our thought quite perfect. (Du Bois 1968:61)

William Edward Burghardt Du Bois was born on February 23, 1868, in the small town of Great Barrington, Massachusetts. His father, Alfred Du Bois, arrived in Western Massachusetts at the age of forty-two. He met Mary Sylvina Burghardt, embarked on a whirlwind relationship, and they were married soon after. They were still trying to figure out where they would settle when their first and only child, Willie, was born. This all took place in just over three years (Lewis 1993). The courtship, never sanctioned by the Burghardt family, meant that the marriage began with an air of tension and disagreement (Du Bois 1968, Lewis 1994). Du Bois relates the story of his parents with a combination of oral history, his own recollections as a child, and probably a bit of biographical license mixed in. He remembered the controversy as a condition of his father being very handsome and phenotypically "too light" for the Burghardt's liking (Du Bois 1968). Biographer David Levering Lewis characterizes this tension as being more rooted in the fact that Alfred Du Bois was an outsider with no real ties to any known New England family (1994).

> When my father came to Great Barrington in 1867, the Black Burghardts did not like him. He was too good-looking, too white. He had apparently no property and no job, so far as they knew; and they had never heard of the Du Bois family in New York. Then suddenly in a runaway marriage, but one duly attested and published by the *Berkshire Courier*, Alfred married Mary Burghardt and they went to live in the house of Jefferson McKinley. Here they lived for a year or two and against them the Black Burghardt family carried a more or less open feud, until my birth. (Du Bois 1968:72)

Soon after Du Bois's birth, Alfred and Mary were no longer together. Du Bois remembers that his father left to find a place for the family to live and not being able to persuade Mary to leave her home and family, as a result, Alfred never returned and Du Bois would never see his father again. His relationship with his father's people was fragile and ensured that he would always have a cursory knowledge about his paternal history. Although there was a clear imbalance, he never gave up pursuing stories from both sides of his family; however, it is hard to say how much of an impact the Du Bois ancestral line had on the shaping of his identity. His life and rearing among the Burghardt clan (as he often described them) was the main source for the shaping of the man he would become. His identity was essentially northern: "In general thought and conduct I became quite thoroughly New England. It was not good form in Great Barrington to express one's thought volubly, or to give way to excessive emotion. We were even sparing in our daily greetings" (Du Bois 1986: 566). He also understood his own maternal family from a class perspective. He describes Great Barrington as not having such a huge distinction between the rich and the poor. "Living was cheap and there was little real poverty" (Du Bois 1968: 79). The Burghardts early on supported themselves on little farms of a few acres and as town laborers and servants. The main "criterion of local social standing was property and ancestry" (Du Bois 1968:80). "They were usually ordinary folk of solid responsibility, farm owners, or artisans merging into industry. Standing did not depend on what the ancestor did, or who he was, but rather that he existed, lived decently and thus linked the individual to the community" (1968:80).

Nestled deep in the Berkshires, on the edge of the South Egremont Plain, was the maternal home of the Burghardt clan. "These Burghardts lived on South Egremont Plain for near 200 years.... Here in the late eighteenth and early nineteenth centuries the black Burghardts lived. I remember three houses and a small pond. These were the homes of Harlow and Ira; and of my own grandfather, Othello, which he had inherited from his sister Lucinda" (Du Bois 1968: 62). Although Du Bois was born in the town of Great Barrington, after the demise of his parents' marriage, he and his mother Mary came to live with his maternal grandparents, Othello and Sally Burghardt. "For a time I lived in the country at the house of my grandfather, Othello, one of three farming brothers. It was sturdy, small and old-fashioned" (Du Bois 1986:562). He always called this place the "house of the Black Burghardts," and I see this place as one of the only places where he was able to be a child. Let me explain. He often describes Great Barrington as "a boy's paradise," with mountains to climb and rivers to swim in, lakes to freeze and hills for coasting (Du Bois 1986:563). However, when he left South Egremont Plain, he had to support his mother physically, mentally and financially. The laughter, lightness and being entwined in the close kinship circle with his maternal family stayed in that space. For Du Bois, the house of the Black Burghardts was his *homeplace*, the place that had a significant impact on his identity and cultural formation. For although he lived at the site for only four brief years, between the ages of 2 and 6, he was a child, absorbing all the information around

Figure 4.1: "House of the Black Burghardts." *The Crisis*, April 1928.
(University of Massachusetts Amherst, Special Collections.)

Figure 4.2:
Mary Burghardt
Du Bois and
W. E. B. Du Bois
as an infant.
(University of
Massachusetts
Amherst, Special
Collections.)

him, his surroundings and memories of family and neighbors. From the age of 6 on, his life was changed, his responsibilities increased, and his path laid by the most influential woman he ever knew, his mother Mary Sylvinia.

Mary Burghardt was described as silent, determined and very patient (Du Bois 1986). Du Bois described his mother as "brown and rather small with smooth skin and lovely eyes, and hair that curled and crinkled down each side of her forehead from the part in the middle" (Du Bois 1986: 561). She was born at Great Barrington on January 14, 1831. She had her first son, Adelbert, at the age of 30. Du Bois remembers Adelbert being born from a union of Mary and a cousin, John. Biographer David Levering Lewis, however, writes that Mary may have ventured out of the security of her insular family and had Adelbert out of wedlock, an affair that would have been more scandalous than having a tryst with a cousin (one with an established family and connection to the area and clan) (Lewis 1994). A few years later, Mary met Alfred and married and gave birth to William Edward in 1868. It seems that Mary's personality and New England roots never allowed her the pleasure of extreme expression and so she silently worried and worried and in many ways affected her own health.

After the death of his grandfather Othello Burghardt, Du Bois and his mother moved back to town, on South Main Street in some rooms over the stables on the Sumner estate. Soon after, Sally Burghardt passed away and they once again moved, this time to a location just down a long lane from the school. Du Bois felt that this was one of the main reasons why his mother chose this location (Du Bois 1968). Soon after this move, Mary had a paralytic stroke, from which she never recovered.

> By the time I neared high school, economic problems and questions of the future began to loom. These were partly settled by my own activities. My mother was then a widow with limited resources of income through boarding the barber, my uncle; supplemented infrequently by day's work, and by some kindly but unobtrusive charity. But I was keen and eager to eke out this income by various jobs: splitting kindling, mowing lawns, doing chores. My first regular wage began as I entered the high school: I went early of mornings and filled with coal one or two of the new so-called 'base-burning' stoves in the millinery shop of Madame L'Hommedieu. (Du Bois 1986: 562)

Du Bois had many responsibilities from the age of 6 to 16, when he finished school. His loyalty to his mother was manifest in many ways. First, was her push for his education and, ultimately, his upward mobility. There were several factors as described by David Levering Lewis about the economic shifts that were happening all around Western Massachusetts. Among them were the influx of European immigrants, often hired by the newly built mills; a decrease in agricultural power; and even the service industry was feeling the push from these new immigrants. African Americans were feeling the effects of a changing America. Du Bois would come of age at a time when one of the only options was the pursuit of education. In many ways, Mary Burghardt was ahead of her time. She realized early in Willie Du Bois's life that his success meant finding a way out of Great Barrington through the path of education, the one place where African Americans could experience a form of "equality" and forward thinking.

Thinking critically about the house of the Black Burghardts, I no longer saw it as a space where he spent four short years; instead, I began to think about the small plot of land as the center of the story, before Du Bois attended Fisk, before he became the first person of African descent to graduate from Harvard, or founding member of the Niagra Movement and the NAACP. This small plot was the *homeplace* of W. E. B. Du Bois in every sense of the word. Du Bois's description of growing up among a family of farmers was initially confusing, because the homesite was only about three tenths of an acre. Then I thought about the connected relationship between the three Burghardt brothers and how close their houses were to each other, and it reminded me of my experiences at the Hermitage Plantation and that complex household. I then saw a different picture of Du Bois's *homeplace*. These farming brothers—Harlow, Ira and Othello—created the playground and the place where young boys and girls of the next Burghardt generation would play and experience a life in a secure, safe and insulated space quite separate from the realities of racial and class distinctions.

Who was W. E. B. Du Bois? He was thoroughly New England, influenced by his family's history, buoyed by his mother's determination, and shaped by his childhood experiences. So, when I set out to write about the early life of Du Bois, I had to focus on the moments of his life often unnoticed in the larger narrative of the Du Bois we know as prolific scholar and writer, activist, public intellectual, teacher, organizer, and Pan-Africanist. My hope here is to unravel a part of his life narrative that centers on the place and the people of his birth and childhood, and highlight the narrative of the women that were such an integral part of his family history and the shaping of the man he would become.

Du Bois, Black Feminist Archaeology
and the Veil of Black Womanhood

If a woman's place is in the home, how do we explain the history of women of African descent in the United States? From the moment we set foot on the shores of the Americas, our worth was defined by the work of our bodies.

> Black women's work took place within two distinct spheres that were at the same time mutually reinforcing and antagonistic. One workplace was centered in their own homes and communities, the locus of family feeling. Beginning in the slave era, the family obligations of wives and mothers overlapped in the area of community welfare, as their desire to nurture their own kin expanded out of the private realm and into public activities that advanced the interests of black people as a group. In contrast to this type of work, which earned for black women the respect of their own people, participation in the paid labor force (or slave economy) reinforced their subordinate status as women and as blacks within American society. Because of their doubly disadvantaged status, black women were confined to two types of work that seemed ironically contradictory—the first was domestic and institutional service, vindictively termed women's work; the other was manual labor so physically arduous it was usually considered men's work. (Jones 1985:3)

The captive African woman had to learn the meaning of work at multiple levels. To survive a system based on free labor, to provide nurturing and support for her family and community, and to learn ways to supplement nothing. In a state like Massachusetts, where the institution of slavery lost its legal sanction in 1783, I had to look beyond my initial understanding of African American women's work in the eighteenth and nineteenth centuries. Initially, my experiences had only been trying to understand the cultural production taking place on the plantation landscape and how captive African women performed as culture bearers and community partners tangled within a "controlled" plantation context. So, shifting to the Northeast and an early "free" state like Massachusetts has not been easy. I had to think in a way that was unfamiliar. My initial reactions to learning of how Mary Burghardt pushed her son toward education and uplift was that his "New Englandness" must have meant she gave him a false sense of racial and social consciousness, that she set him up to think of himself as better than all around him. This was not the case. As I continued to learn about Blackness in Massachusetts, I realized that young Willie Du Bois became the means for his mother to break through the boundaries of a social situation that she did not see herself able to overcome. It was through him that she could alter the stagnating and isolated path that her life, despite her possible desires, had unfortunately taken. She wanted her son to become more than the Burghardt men around him; she wanted him to be able to move beyond the economic and class boundaries set by their race, class and (for Mary) gender. I believe, honestly, that she wanted him to leave Great Barrington and never look back, and after her death that is exactly what he did.

At an early age Du Bois was beginning to recognize the reality of class distinctions, which when combined with race created a very distinct identity process for him. He knew he was different, but not by the same means as if he had grown up in the southern United States. As Du Bois describes it:

> The social classes of the town were built partly on landholding farmers and more especially on manufacturers and merchants, whose property was due in no little degree to the new and high tariff. The rich people of the town were not very rich nor many in number. The middle class were farmers, merchants and artisans; and beneath these was a small proletariat of Irish and German mill workers. They lived in slums near the woolen mills and across the river clustering about the Catholic Church. The number of colored people in the town and county was small. They were all, save directly after the war, old families, well-known to the old settlers among the whites. The color line was manifest and yet not absolutely drawn. (Du Bois 1986: 560)

When we include the category of gender, these intersecting oppressions complicate the larger discussion of domestic space, women's suffrage, labor rights and the African American experience. As I sit in my office writing, I often look on my walls to see two posters and one picture, all of which have followed me through many adventures and places. The posters are of two women, Old Hannah and Betty, who were born into captivity at the Hermitage and lived long enough to experience freedom. For me, they serve as reminders of the people I write for, the stakeholders that keep me honest with myself and the work I hope to continue. The photo is of my great-grandmother, Hattie Shaw Goodwyn, who was always known as Gram, my great-aunt Oda, and my great-uncles Percy and William. Gram reminds me of the complexity of identity and family histories, how they shape and confuse and give strength all at the same time. I think about the difficulty of writing and expressing in a passionate, yet thoughtful way, and think twice about the expectations I have set for myself. Especially when I think about how the bodies of these women, how their hands and what they produced (in many ways) is what defined them. As I look closer to the pictures, I see their hands bent with arthritic pain, bones brittle from hard labor, hard lives; their eyes tired of seeing (as my grandmother would say) before light to after dark. Yet the most telling feature they share is that although their backs seem like they should be brittle with age and effort, they sit and stand so straight and purposeful. This goes beyond strength; it speaks to their patience and their ability to continue to exist for a larger purpose. These moments are when I not only see me, I think of the work of W. E. B. Du Bois in his most formative years, in Great Barrington, among the Burghardt family, surrounded by women of purpose, women that never left his consciousness.

This is why when I began my relationship with the Boyhood Homesite, I saw gender all over the project. Even Du Bois remembers the impact of these Burghardt women in his life.

As I remember through memories of others, backward among my own family, it is the mother of my grandmothers, who sobbed her life away in song, longing for her lost palm-trees and scented waters; the tall and bronzed grandmother, with beaked nose and shrewish eyes, who loved and scolded her black and laughing husband as he smoked lazily in his high oak chair; above all, my own mother, with all of her soft brownness, —the brown velvet of her skin, the sorrowful black-brown eyes, and the tiny brown-capped waves of her midnight hair as it lay new parted on her forehead. All the way back in these dim distances it is mothers and mothers of mothers who seem to count, while fathers are shadowy memories. (Du Bois 1986: 955)

Du Bois was concerned about women, our neglect in the larger argument of freedom of all peoples of African descent. It was about the brutality of capture, the inhumanity of captivity, the false promise of freedom, all of which were compromised by the contradictory nature of Black womanhood and motherhood. "As I look about me today in this veiled world of mine, despite the noisier and more spectacular advance of my brothers, I instinctively feel and know that it is the five million women of my race who really count" (Du Bois 1986: 963).

Ellen Irene Diggs was an African American pioneer in the field of anthropology, and my first introduction to how passionate Du Bois was concerning the rights of women of African descent. She is best known for her work on African influences in Latin America, especially in Cuba, where she worked closely with Cuban anthropologist Fernando Ortiz (Bolles 1999). While working on a graduate degree at Atlanta University, she met and began working as a research assistant for W. E. B. Du Bois. She continued to work with him for more than eleven years, on such seminal works as *Black Reconstruction in America, 1860-1880* (1935), *Black Folk, Then and Now* (1939), *Dusk of Dawn* (1940), and *The Encyclopedia of the Negro* (1945) (Bolles 1999:158). Patricia Morton described the tension Du Bois suffered trying to produce so much work while not having the time or ability to complete all the research he wanted. I describe this as a form of suffering because it was difficult and time consuming to follow his own methods and not rely on the racist historical imagery and work of Euroamerican historians. He leaned heavily on Black historians who often saw the stereotypical images of slavery as destroying the family and men as having no power and being categorized as "guests in the house" as unrealistic (Morton 1991: 58). He also leaned heavily on research assistants like Irene Diggs to conduct critical information gathering and fact checking. In shaping my discussion of Black Feminist Archaeology at a site known primarily for its association with a great male figure W. E. B. Du Bois, I began to seriously contemplate why this was such a plausible way to interpret his life. As I started to learn the larger history of the site and his childhood, I learned of the essential role of the Burghardt women, especially his mother Mary.

While revisiting A. Lynn Bolles's biographical essay on Irene Diggs, I found the material. I found through her words the essays in which he spoke of women, their struggles and the undying love he had for his mother. It was the beginning of my understanding of Du Bois's brand of "Black feminism."

> Because Du Bois was aware of the way in which suffrage for women was interlocked with suffrage for blacks he was an early, consistent, constant advocate of women's suffrage. Every argument for Negro suffrage, he said, was an argument for woman's suffrage; every argument for woman suffrage is an argument for Negro suffrage. He predicted that the struggle for woman suffrage would lead to widespread discussion of Negro suffrage, North and South. (Diggs 1974:279)

Du Bois used *The Crisis* as a means for bringing to the forefront issues of discrimination, feminist causes, premier women writers, and to condemn America's abuse of Black women—economic, sexual, psychological and physical (Morton 1991:56–57). Du Bois's arguments are similar to those of contemporary Black Feminist scholars because of the way he describes the complexity of an oppression based on race, gender and class. In his words:

> For this, their promise, and for their hard past, I honor the women of my race. Their beauty —their dark and mysterious beauty of midnight eyes, crumpled hair, and soft, full-featured faces—is

perhaps more to me than to you, because I was born to its warm and subtle spell; but their worth is yours as well as mine. No other women on earth could have emerged and from the hell of force and temptation which once engulfed and still surrounds black women in America with half the modesty and womanliness that they retain. (Du Bois [1920] 1986: 968)

In his words I see the only logical conclusion: it is not only for myself and future generations of women of African descent that I write; I also write for Du Bois, in the sense of a contemporary Black Feminist who has seen the beauty of his words and now understands the importance of telling the story of the Burghardt women.

Some Stories of the Burghardt Clan

The black Burghardts were a group of African Negroes descended from Tom, who was born in West Africa about 1730. He was stolen by Dutch slave traders and brought to the valley of the Hudson as a small child. Legally, Tom was not a slave, but practically, by the custom of the day, he grew up as either a slave or serf, and in the serve of the Burghardts, a white family of Dutch descent. Early in the 18th century, 'Coonraet Borghardt' and Tom came east from the Hudson Valley and settled in Berkshire County, Massachusetts, which was described as a 'howling wilderness.' (Du Bois 1968: 62)

The Black Burghardts lived on South Egermont Plain for nearly 200 years (Du Bois 1968). In this location marriages happened, children were born and raised, food was grown, and family was preserved. This land held social importance for the Burghardt clan, for it was on South Egremont Plain that they lived and left behind the material that will ultimately help archaeologists such as myself tell the story of Black life in Western Massachusetts. As I peeled back the layers of the Burghardt family narrative, I found names of people whom I initially thought of as marginal in the story as very important to the site. Nearly 200 years is a long time to chronicle, and in trying to understand the history of property, I quickly began to recognize how nearly every member of the family mattered in some way. This is how I came to know Thomas, Maria and Lucinda.

Jacob and Violet Burghardt had six children: Ira, Harlow, Othello, Thomas, Lucinda and Maria. Of this generation, three of the six worked in some capacity for the Kellogg family, a Euroamerican family of some means from Great Barrington. The story of these two families is a long one, but one that speaks volumes to the subtle and in many ways invisible experiences of people of African descent in New England. The relationship, historically, is viewed as more of a reciprocal relationship than may have been the reality. This illusive, yet complicated relationship between families included land transactions, domestic service, and what has been interpreted as great charity. However, as I continued to read the memories of Du Bois and the histories by David Levering Lewis and Bernard Drew, coupling them with my new understanding of the details of some of the family stories of Black New Englanders, I began to see more clearly that these relationships were fraught with inconsistencies and contradictions. To be of African descent from New England was more complex than being legally freed in 1783. There remained an assumption that Blackness meant servitude, and servitude meant that one would eventually benefit materially or socially from these connections; but freedom was still not free, even in the seat of abolitionist New England.

The story of Thomas, Maria and Lucinda is fascinating. It is filled with challenges to the utopian belief of the egalitarian nature of the Northeast. It does, however, reflect the reality of race, class, labor and choice. Thomas and Maria went to work for Ezra Kellogg, Esq., "who came to town about 1775 and eventually married Mary Whiting. As deputy sheriff, he narrowly eluded seizure by a mob of irate farmers during an episode of Shay's Rebellion" (Drew 1999:369). In 1832 Sarah Kellogg, one of the daughters of Ezra Kellogg, started a young ladies' boarding school in the old town Central School, where the St. James Episcopal Church now stands (Drew 1999: 351). Sarah, her twin Mary and younger sister Nancy operated this school, that evolved into the Rose Cottage Seminary, until 1853 (Drew 1999:334).

Drew continues, "After Mr. Kellogg's death, Tom was the faithful servant at Rose Cottage, where Misses Kellogg continued their school; and still kept with them in their retirement, till taken to his final resting place last Sabbath.... Nobody heard him complain his lot, or utter the least murmur" (1999:369).

Thomas's story is incredibly documented by Great Barrington historian Bernard Drew:

> When Burghardt died at the age of seventy-five, he earned, not an obituary, but a long letter of tribute, unsigned, which described him as 'a fortunate and happy man beyond most of the colored race. I first knew him as the hired man of Ezra Kellogg Esq. of this village; and his term of service in that family has lasted over fifty years.... There was nothing of eye-service about Tom, as he was familiarly called. He was an enemy of all alcoholic drinks, and a steady adherent to the temperance cause. He never used tobacco in any form. He was always found in his place at the Sabbath.' (1999: 369)

The story of Tom's sister Maria seemed to be a little more fortunate in some ways. She did find love and companionship by marrying Samuel Van Ness, another in the employ of the Kellogg family. They never had children; however, it seems she lived a full and long life. Although a majority of the lives of Thomas and Maria happened away from the Burghardt land, I believe they always factored into the Burghardt story, for they were among the success stories of the day and in many ways added to the overall social standing of the Burghardt descendants, in the manner of being associated with an established and well-respected Euroamerican family.

Drew believes that the dedication to Maria Burghardt Van Ness was probably penned by Nancy Kellogg, it was overflowing with emotion and for me was just as telling:

> Mrs. Maria Van Ness...was born in Great Barrington, daughter of John (Jacob) Burghardt, sister of Mr. Thomas Burghardt, who for so many years was known in this village as 'Tommy,' and who was universally respected for his pure and honest life....

Her parents were slaves. At the age of thirty-two, she entered the family of Ezra Kellogg, Esq. and had remained with his children ever since her position of servant, but with the spirit of a friend. She became so identified with household experiences, the changes, the joys and sorrows and had become by her helpfulness and sympathy so much a part of the family that her death seems more like the loss of a sister than the departure of a servant.... She died, peacefully, after a long and disagreeable illness, in the 73rd year of her age. (Drew 1999: 369)

Du Bois also remembers the story of Tom, "One uncle became a lifelong servant of the Kellogg family, and the legend was that his unpaid wages kept that family from suffering until one daughter married the man who helped build the Pacific Railroad" (Du Bois 1968:64). This is how the family remembered "Tommy," as working his whole life for the Kellogg family without pay and without the opportunity to marry, have children, or perhaps benefit from the company of his larger extended family. Much later, after their sister Lucinda became a widow and was legally blind, she moved in to spend the remainder of her days in service of the Kellogg sisters. In reading about these relationships, the Kellogg family are often remembered as benevolent and even charitable (in the case of Lucinda) to all members of the Burghardt family; however, this level of servitude is still reminiscent of captivity in many ways. It brings to the surface that choices for people of African descent were limited and often quite lasting. However tragic these lifelong relationships were, they proved to be important in the story of the homesite property. For it was Lucinda Burghardt Freeman who passed the property down to her three brothers, Ira, Harlow and Othello, who then lived for years on the property.

This is one of many personal stories of the Burghardt family. Du Bois talked about the types of occupations his family pursued:

In my family, I remember farmers, barbers, waiter, cooks, housemaids and laborers. In these callings a few prospered. My cousins, the Crispels of West Stockbridge, owned one of the best homes in town, and had the only barber shop; my Uncle Jim long had a paying barber business in Amherst; several hotel cooks and waiters were in charge of dining rooms, did well and were held in esteem; a cousin in Lenox was a sexton in the most prominent church, and his wife and four daughters ran an exclusive laundry; the family was well-to-do, but they worked hard and unceasingly. (1968: 63)

During the period of the Great Migration, which spanned from about 1917 to 1970, about 7 million African Americans left the South to live in cities across the North and Midwest (Wilkerson 2010). However, before the Emancipation Proclamation, issued in 1863, began the elimination of captivity nationally, Massachusetts had outlawed the institution within its borders in 1783 (Paynter 2001, Piper & Levinson 2010). This large gap in time meant that many escapees traveled to the Bay state in search of freedom and a chance to carve out a new life. With captivity illegal, the long history of abolition, and the multiple stations of the Underground Railroad, Massachusetts was a logical place to settle for many new escapees. In the recollections of Du Bois, he often describes, to varying degrees, some fissures in the relationships between different generations of people of African descent—between the "settled" families and the new arrivals. In the Berkshires, even further removed from the city centers like Boston or Springfield, tourism and the second home industries pulled people from all over to work as hotel domestics, waiters, and other service trades. Du Bois described the breakdown of non-Euroamerican Berkshire folk:

In Great Barrington there were perhaps twenty-five, certainly not more than fifty, colored folk in a population of five thousand. My family was among the oldest inhabitants of the valley. The family had spread slowly through the county intermarrying among cousins and other black folk with some but limited infiltration of white blood. Other dark families had come in and there was some intermingling with local Indians. In one or two cases there were groups of apparently later black immigrants, near Sheffield for instance. There survives even to this day an isolated group of black folk whose origin in obscure. We knew little of them but felt above them because of our education and economic status. ([1940] 1986)

There remained a clear distinction between the "later black immigrants" and the Burghardts and other established families. It is an analysis of tensions like these that has become the topic for how we as archaeologists engage with the local community. Conflict and class distinctions can be pressure points, but they can also provide, for younger generations, details about history that they have never considered. These issues become a part of an incredible and sustainable dialogue that bridges the generations, various racialized communities, and people beyond the Berkshire county boundary.

In reading Du Bois biographer David Levering Lewis's historic work on Du Bois's life, we get the sense of the extreme poverty and the quick downfall of the Burghardt family. This was the case for Du Bois and his mother, who had a paralytic stroke that impaired the use of her left leg and possibly her left arm (Lewis 1993:29). This stroke made it virtually impossible for her to work beyond small chores and odd jobs. This was a very difficult time for young Willie. Not only was he living in a small and cramped apartment on Railroad Street, but it was a time where he came into direct contact with working class Irish and German immigrants that he may not have had much contact with prior. Du Bois began to understand firsthand how the increased presence of a larger labor pool was changing the economic circumstances for African Americans in the late nineteenth and early twentieth centuries. There was a boom of mills and factories springing up across the state; however, they were only hiring European immigrants, which left a huge decline in the prospects for employment opportunities for people of African descent (Lewis 1994). Du Bois looked at his past with a nostalgia and veiled shame (Muller 2001:36). There were aspects of his childhood that I think caused him to be sad and angry about the lot dealt the Burghardt family, especially the men. The hardships that these men faced considering exclusionary industrialization, excessively competitive agriculture, and lack of educational and economic opportunity, led him to read not just race as a factor in his family's precarious social situation, but class as a factor for exclusionary practices on a variety of levels. It was here that he really developed the sense of class distinctions (Lewis 1994). So, the Great Barrington that Du Bois never forgot had hard lessons to learn and the personal stories of these hardships and triumphs in his young life. These are among the personal stories that I think make our work relevant and compelling across generations, race and class. It paints a human picture of who Du Bois was and serves as a background for the archaeology ahead.

Archaeology at the House of the Black Burghardts

Stories are beginning to emerge from the archaeology conducted at the W.E.B. Du Bois Boyhood Homesite, as well as from the documents. In spring of 1982 Homer (Skip) Meade, then a lecturer in the W.E.B. Du Bois Department of Afro-American Studies, and Ernest Allen, chair of the department, approached a brand new assistant professor of anthropology, Robert Paynter, to ask if he thought historical archaeology might have a role to play in enhancing Du Bois's legacy at the University of Massachusetts Amherst. The campus, under the leadership of Chancellor Randolph Bromery, had recently acquired Du Bois's papers. Skip Meade was especially interested in seeing the property that had been purchased by Dr. Edmund Gordon and Walter Wilson in 1967 to develop a memorial dedicated to Du Bois become a place where Du Bois's memory could be appropriately honored. As Bob relates it, "I had a very vague recognition of Du Bois's name and told Skip and Ernie I thought so and would get back to them. Spending only the briefest time with Julius Lester's splendid biography and compilation of Du Bois's writings made clear to me that, yes, I very much wanted to do whatever I could to have archaeology at the Homesite contribute to Du Bois's legacy" (personal communication 2011). Thus began three field schools of archaeology at the Homesite.

Paynter and his students and colleagues have presented some of this work in publications, professional presentations, and even an exhibit at the State House in Boston (Paynter 1990,1992, 1997, 2001; Paynter et al. 1994; Paynter et al. 2005). Not surprisingly, given Bob's record of bringing a race-class-gender analysis to historical archaeology, such an approach can be found in these studies, one that allows us to work together in a productive scholarly back-and-forthing. I am also very much indebted to the work of Nancy Muller (2001), whose dissertation not only clarified the elements of Du Bois's genealogy and the deed chain for the Homesite, but was also a prescient womanist approach to the history of the Du Bois Boyhood Homesite.

The stories of these field schools are embedded in a history of struggle to develop an appropriate commemoration to Du Bois, one that I am proud to say I am "lineally" related to, as it was the father of one of my key mentors at Texas, Dr. Edmund Gordon, who had the foresight with Walter Wilson to purchase the Du Bois Boyhood Homesite in 1967 and preserve it. Professor William Strickland of the W. E. B. Du Bois Department of Afro-American Studies at the UMass Amherst played a major role in transferring the Homesite to the stewardship of the University. As I am writing this Bob is putting the finishing touches on a site report for all the work conducted at the 1983, 1984 and 2003 field schools (http://scholarworks.umass.edu/du_bois_boyhood_survey/). To date the archaeology has cataloged some 30,000 artifacts, clarified property issues related to the Homesite, and raised intriguing questions that we intend to pursue in future archaeology.

Many lines of study are emerging as I become more familiar with this collection. One of the most intriguing involves why the W.E.B. Du Bois Boyhood Homesite, a National Landmark property, requires the services of archaeologists. As noted above, Du Bois lived at the Homesite with his mother and her parents when he was a youth, between 1870 and 1874. He was given the Homesite as a sixtieth birthday present in 1928. The House of the Black Burghardts was purchased from some of his relatives in a state of disrepair. Although Du Bois attempted to restore the House, his funds were insufficient for the task, with the approaching Great Depression and his work at *The Crisis*. A very dilapidated house was pushed to the back of the lot when it was sold to Du Bois's neighbors in 1954, to lie dormant until the efforts by Gordon and Wilson to revive the site in 1967.

Hence the need for archaeology, to identify and outline the location of the House, to study the uses of the homelot, and to cope with the thousands of artifacts scattered on and just below the surface in the area where the House was pushed to. Interestingly, the artifact assemblage associated with the House dates to the late nineteenth and very early twentieth century, the period of occupation by Lena and Edward Wooster and their four children. And the thousands of artifacts, mostly from the surface, represent every aspect of daily life, including ink wells, shoes, plates, cups, saucers, tea cups, jars, utensils, coal, and furniture hardware. So, this assemblage poses a question: why did the Wooster family seemingly so precipitously abandon so many of its worldly belongings in the early twentieth century?

As I began to comb through the documents and read through the stories and recollections of the site and its history, I thought about one possible scenario to explain the sudden exodus of the family. The Woosters most likely parted ways sometime between 1915 and

Figure 4.3: An assortment of artifacts from the W. E. B. Du Bois Boyhood Homesite. (Photo courtesy of Christopher Douyard.)

1917. This is when the House appears to have been abandoned. This had remained a question for years; we were trying to understand the circumstances behind the Woosters' exit. Then I began to read the incredible dissertation of Nancy Muller (2001), who painstakingly combed through the historic background of the site using Du Bois's words and memory as a guide. Prior to the Woosters' tenure at the site, it appears to have been in the hands of descendants of Harlow Burghardt, a Martha Burghardt Piper and her daughter Louise Burghardt Brown, of Philadelphia, Pennsylvania. There is a transaction between the women and a George Taylor, who has one-third of a larger property (.3 acres), which he sells to Lena Wooster for one dollar in 1909. The couple, married in 1907, had several children. which were all listed in the 1910 census as living at the Boyhood Homesite. The Woosters occupy the property from 1909 until 1917, when the marriage seems to split up and the couple goes their separate ways. I had to agree with Muller's assessment of the fractured and broken relationship between Edward and Lena Wooster, especially because Muller finds that Edward is still living in Great Barrington with a Maria Hinkley and that Lena has relocated to Springfield, Massachusetts (Muller 2001).

The next reference we have to the property is when Du Bois inquires about the possibility of purchasing the property. In September of 1925, he writes a letter to his cousin, Edward Wooster, who he believes lives in Springfield, Massachusetts, and who he assumes is the owner of the property (Du Bois papers). The property, however, was in the hands of Edward's estranged wife, Lena—who was living on Orleans Street in Springfield—not Edward (Muller 2001).

The archaeology is interesting because it can give us more than just the story of one particular household and one family living within its walls. The artifacts become the words that create a narrative that moves us to look beyond the broken and discarded plates and glasses of a small house on the South Egremont Plain to see the larger implications of the information we learn about the larger life history of the site itself. For me the House of the Black Burghardts becomes the site of family history, a place to decipher the complexity of a figure like W. E. B. Du Bois, and the basis for a larger discussion of Blackness in New England. The House is the physical site of Du Bois's maternal line and provides the means to address interesting issues such as the invisibility of race in New England's historical memory, a way to begin a more grounded dialogue about the philosophy of "double consciousness," and ultimately, the story of Du Bois and women.

The House again becomes the symbol of *homeplace* for Du Bois as a young boy. It was also the first (and possibly last) place where he was fully imbedded within his maternal kinship. Du Bois's quest to understand both his maternal and paternal ancestry is that of a man who was firm in character, yet constantly searching for a true place of belonging. Although Great Barrington served as the foundation of the man he would become, there remained a certain fluidity to his identity making, a subject that he pursued until his last days. From reading the descriptions in *Souls of Black Folk, Darkwater, Dusk of Dawn* or *The Autobiography of W. E. B. Du Bois*, he admits that words and memories change:

> Autobiographies do not form indisputable authorities. They are always incomplete, and often unreliable. Eager as I am to put down the truth, there are difficulties; memory fails especially in small details, so that it becomes finally but a theory of my life, with much forgotten and misconceived, with valuable testimony but often less than absolutely true, despite my intention to be frank and fair. (1968: 12)

Development of a Black Feminist Du Boisian Archaeology

I am completely thankful to the work and legacy of Robert Paynter and his commitment to archaeology and commemoration at the W. E. B. Du Bois Boyhood Homesite in Great Barrington, Massachusetts. Through his excavations, artifact interpretation, community connections, and commitment to seeing the site fulfill all of its possibilities, I have found myself in the most perfect place as a young and excited archaeologist. It is the dream of a lifetime to be able to decide where to make your research home. When the opportunity to make UMass Amherst my real and intellectual home, I realized there were greater powers at work here, for I could not have chosen a better project site, a more supportive anthropology department, and such incredible colleagues and engaged graduate and undergraduate students. This is what brought my family and me to Western Massachusetts. So, as I step into the Du Bois archaeology project alongside Bob Paynter, not only do I continue to learn from him, but learn with him—about the next steps, the ways to adapt to the changing needs of the community, the discipline, and the world around us.

In anthropology there is an underlying philosophy that challenges cultural anthropologists to think critically about their own subject position to ensure that personal views do not alter perception of people different from themselves. I therefore challenge archaeologists to keep the elements of critical self analysis when engaging with sites of Africans in the Americas. When we take for granted our andro- and Eurocentric worldview we can miss new and exciting ways of reading the subtleness of documents, miss finding the invisible stories of people who never enter into the written dialogue and whose material culture becomes the only means of their historical presence. So, when historical archaeologists continue to use the same tools to simplify the African past in the Americas in ways that are comfortable and safe, we do not recognize how the double and triple burdens of oppression (race, gender and class) could open up a conversation that considers the lives and experiences of a multitude of marginalized people in the past and the present.

There are very interesting lines of inquiry that could include why and how the Burghardt women wielded so much power in a time when that was not commonplace. There were clear decisions about property and inheritance that were made and maintained by these women. These details are not insignificant, but essential to the shaping of the research questions that could prove to be relevant to local stakeholders and scholars outside of African Diaspora archaeology. We will not be ignoring the little nuances of the lives of women of

Figure 4.4: Signage of current trail at Du Bois Boyhood Homesite.
(Photo courtesy of Rachel Fletcher.)

African descent; we will bring them to the forefront of the questions we ask and how we view the details of our own archaeological methods. Why shouldn't a site as significant as the Du Bois Boyhood Homesite bring up and display the everyday lives of women and men of African descent and place them both at the center of interpretive models? Especially because if they were as important as I believe they were, this approach is essential to a discussion of the Homesite, Du Bois's life, and a study of Black life in the Berkshires.

The future of archaeology at the Homesite includes more than laying out grids, excavating units, drawing maps, and collecting artifacts. The methodology we are engaged with is enmeshed within an astounding set of social relations. We are working directly with the newly established Du Bois Center at UMass Amherst and Director of Marketing Brooks Fitch as the starting point of our growing social network. With a range of scholars from across campus, such as William Strickland and Amilcar Shabazz, chair of the W. E. B. Du Bois Department of Afro-American Studies; David Glassberg and Barbara Krauthamer of the History Department; Jay Schafer, Director of UMass Libraries; and Robert Cox and Danielle Kovacs, also of the library. Beyond campus, our network expands into Great Barrington to include the Friends of the Du Bois Boyhood Homesite, including members Rachel Fletcher, Bernie Drew, Elaine Gunn, Wray Gunn and Cora Portnoff (also of Clinton African Methodist Zion Church) and other friends that continue to add to our dialogue, like Delores Root, architect Michael Singer, designer Veronica Jackson and Lonnie Bunch of the African American Museum of History and Culture. These networks have created lively dialogues, passionate debates and an incredible archaeological project ahead of us.

Conclusion

There is a need in historical archaeology for a larger discussion of how archaeologists fall prey to recreating the culture of poverty model without intending to. With the quest to tell a hidden story, interpreting the material past often becomes tangled within the reality of contemporary perceptions of race and class in US society. There is also no honest discussion that addresses how archaeological interpretation should navigate misconceptions about poverty, broken families, and other modern notions of social and political ills. These are real. They have been, in my opinion, in the background of African American and African Diaspora archaeology. However, an engaged historical archaeology is one that not only recognizes these glaring silences, but addresses them as well. Initially, I feared how my interpretation highlighting the role of women within the Black Domestic Sphere would be received. As I directly confront aspects of a culture of poverty model, mythological notions of Black pathological culture, and then relate it to the false connection between captivity and current racialized issues (for example see Moynihan Report 1965). However, the sad truth is that I am assuming a lot about historical archaeology and its connection with the African

American past. Some of what I have just described remains as nuanced details about African American history that exist in a parallel universe, never to be fully incorporated into the field of archaeology. I want to positively confront the canon that many of us rely on, and push for the inclusion of the Black literary tradition and ways to tell the personal stories of the people who occupied the sites we excavate. There should be more than an assumption; there should be a way for archaeology to interact or converse with the historical assumptions about slavery, the Black family, Black women, Black labor (especially Black women's labor) and the larger implications for people living today.

CHAPTER V

Moving Mountains and Liberating Dialogues

....

As women, we have been taught to either ignore our differences or to view them as causes for separation and suspicion rather than as forces for change. Without community, there is no liberation, only the most vulnerable and temporary armistice between an individual and her oppression. But community must not mean a shedding of our differences, nor the pathetic pretense that these differences do not exist. Those of us who stand outside the circle of this society's definition of acceptable women; those of us who have been forged in the crucibles of difference; those of us who are poor, who are lesbians, who are black, who are older, know that survival is not an academic skill. It is learning how to stand alone, unpopular and sometimes reviled, and how to make common cause with those others identified as outside the structures, in order to define and seek a world in which we can all flourish. It is learning how to take our differences and make them strengths. For the master's tools will never dismantle the master's house. They may allow us temporarily to beat him at his own game, but they will never enable us to bring about genuine change. And this fact is only threatening to those women who still define the master's house as their only source of support.

Audre Lorde, "The Master's Tools Will Never Dismantle the Master's House," comments at "The Personal and the Political" Panel, Second Sex Conference, October 1979

Write the book you want to write, for the people you want to write for, because if you don't do it now, you will carry those words around like cumbersome baggage that will never fit in the overhead bin or underneath the seat in front of you. And when you walk with too much stuff, it weighs you down and our goal is to be light and free from burden…for once in our lives…until the next book forms in your brain.

Whitney Battle-Baptiste, to herself during the process
of writing this book

When I first imagined this book, I thought about titles. I racked my brain for clever phrases or unique ideas. However, I kept coming full circle to the name *Black Feminist Archaeology*. Yet, I feared this title for several reasons. Although it seemed to carry with it a sense of strength, it also carried with it the possibility of alienating several groups of people who may not be able to see beyond those three words together. I did not write a book to push for a theoretical agenda that excludes anyone. I write for an audience that is ready to hear about how race, gender and class complicate the field of archaeology and make it relevant to the larger world. I want this book to show how when archaeologists critically engage with a dialogue about the intersectionality of race and gender, we begin to see the deeper forms of oppression and how they affect the lives of marginalized populations. Through all of my contemplation, I came back to the title, because for me it was the most honest, realistic and simple part of writing the book. *Black Feminist Archaeology* is a title that will live beyond my time and positively contribute to a larger understanding of how we are all connected by time, space, place and event. I want to stress to all who may not think the title speaks to them, do not let Black Feminism scare you away; the reality is that it is the great equalizer.

Within the pages of *Black Feminist Archaeology*, I provide the space for an open and honest dialogue about the intersectionality of race, gender, and class in the story of the American past. I illustrate how a gendered lens can move toward a complex and layered analysis of the lives of African women, men and children in the Americas. I am creating a space that allows for a larger understanding of a methodology that makes it possible for anyone to engage in an inclusive archaeology.

I also want this book to provide the possibility for scholars outside of the discipline of archaeology to see how the strategies used in *Black Feminist Archaeology* can benefit their own theory formation and research methodologies to tell the story of the African past in the Americas. There is value in this approach for other disciplines to see the value of a materially grounded research in ways that only happen in archaeology. This diasporic approach can also expand beyond the borders of the United States, because it has global dimensions. In practice, I believe that intersectional archaeological analysis functions throughout the Caribbean, Central and South America, and the continent of Africa.

To move beyond limits, to see the value of African worldviews in our understanding of the African Diaspora allows us to let go of tragic misconceptions and false judgements that are based on Eurocentric notions of history. Our emphasis on family structures, community responsibilities, gender norms and expectations, and cultural forms of practice and maintenance are all topics that can benefit from an approach like those used in Black Feminist Archaeology.

These approaches have allowed me to ask different types of questions, find alternative sources for the research questions I developed for the sites I have worked with and the material I have analyzed or interpreted. This has allowed me to go to sites like the W. E. B. Du Bois Boyhood Homesite with new questions about family, gender, class, race and labor in ways that are not on the surface, but hidden in the details. It is at the Du Bois Boyhood Homesite that I hope to untangle the complexity of material choices of the Burghardt women, and how gender and labor intersect in complicated and subtle ways.

Since beginning this book project I have begun to more fully understand the ways that time alters how sites and the artifacts we find are interpreted. We do not simply change our opinions and approaches to the material, but we allow for current and contemporary thoughts and approaches to positively influence how we see the past. In other words, is it so terrible for our interpretations of the past to change over time if they continue to help us learn lessons at that moment? I think that sites such as Lucy Foster's Acre and the W. E. B. Du Bois Boyhood Homesite help us in the process of creating new dialogues and conclusions. The Foster site was pivotal for the history of Americanist archaeology in the early 1940s, but the site means so much more to us today. This site encompassed a variety of issues such as race, gender, labor and class at a time when an intersectional approach was not the normal method to analyze a site. Lucy Foster's story also complicates the myth of racial and social equality of the North by helping us to see the restricted lives of freed people like Lucy. Her life story is a part of the picture that makes the work of digging up broken pottery and glass relevant to exchanges between archaeologists and the larger public.

At the Du Bois Boyhood Homesite, we are able to actively bring a Pan Africanist perspective to a Northern place like Great Barrington, Massachusetts. The life and scholarship of W. E. B. Du Bois was global in scope, his work reached people from all backgrounds. It is with this lens that we hope to make the archaeology of the little spot we call his homesite appealing to a broad audience, those that may be familiar with his work and those that may only know his name. The thousands of artifacts are not about his life, but are the story of his family, their legacy and struggles in a place often softened by images of abolitionism and legalized "freedom." The artifacts speak to ideas about poverty, displacement, African American consumerism and property ownership. There are also many stories that can be tied to the site that make for a lifetime of research, outreach and future fieldwork.

There are moments of doubt that a writer has as she comes to the end of a project. For me, I felt it the entire time, on one level or another. I understand that although women make up about 50 percent of archaeologists in the United States, we are not represented in the volumes of edited works published or among faculty at major institutions (Conkey 2007). So, at times my confidence had to be checked, because I was not just proposing general theory, I was pushing for an archaeological theory based in Black Feminist thought. I was never completely sure if the coupling of a theoretical model that encouraged change and the practical approach to the study of archaeological material would come together to reflect both my feelings and experiences, and still be academically acceptable. Yet, in the back of my mind was always the thought that this book was not just for me. It was a project that would stand as a testament, not only to what I was feeling at this moment in my career, but also as a document to stand as testimony to my struggles, the struggles of my ancestor mothers and for my children to look to for answers to complicated and illusive questions they might face one day, about race, gender, archaeology and life as Africans in America.

At the beginning of 2010 I did an interview with the *Bay State Banner* and was asked a very simple, yet compelling question. The question was, "What has been your experience as a person of African descent doing an archaeology of the African Diaspora?" The one thing I did emphasize in my long answer was the fact that it is really not my individual experiences that should be the center of the work that I do; it should be how these experiences shape the approaches and methodological details that I bring to the conversation. It is also about the way that my experience and identity inform my interpretation of theory that can often differ from the status quo or mainstream explanations. So, it is not my authority of "voicing the Other," but more like speaking the unspoken or forgotten. Those small details that allow for a broader perception of the past that moves beyond the basic interpretive framework. As an archaeologist of African descent, I see the value of my discipline as adding a level of complexity to the larger story of African American history, yet I also understand the hesitation of descendant communities to see the value or the necessity of archaeology. It is not disinterest; it is more like distrust. What can the practice of archaeology or archaeological interpretation do for social justice? How can the analysis of artifacts and material culture help us to work toward liberation? What can African Diaspora archaeology offer to the struggle of people of African descent today? At the initial stages of shaping my dissertation and getting to the nuts and bolts of what it is that I was trying to do, one of my mentors,

Ted Gordon, asked me these very questions. It was a short meeting, because I had no answer. I thought I was on this mission to bring archaeology to *my* people. However, what was I offering them? What was I really bringing to the conversation? When I go back to the Bronx, Brooklyn, Texas or Nashville, what is the conversation? Most of the time it has nothing to do with my identity as an archaeologist. For so long I saw my work as a reflection of who I was, but the work I was doing was to get a degree, to get a post-doctoral fellowship, to get a tenure-track position, not social justice or Black liberation. So, that is why I wrote this book. I write this book for my elders, my peers, my children and my community. I know that to write in this way is a risk, but if I do not, how will my work have an impact on the world, or push the discipline, or allow me to tell the stories of my ancestors?

Epilogue: Replacing the Tongs

During my tenure at the Hermitage, I developed what I termed a compound model to try to understand the possible ways in which captive families collectively used space to socialize, find comfort and complete daily needs of their immediate community. At the center of that compound was what I referred to as the hearth, the center of the compound, the heart of the complex household. At the W. E. B. Du Bois Boyhood Homesite, it was no different. The importance of that central place, that gathering place, that one spot that meant comfort and home was true for Du Bois as well.

> It is the first home I remember....I left the house as a child to live in town and go to school. But for furtive glimpses I did not see the house again for more than a quarter century. Then riding near on a chance journey I suddenly was homesick for that house. I came to the spot. There it stood, old, lonesome, empty. Its windowless eyes stare blindly on the broad, black highway to New York.... From that day to this I desperately wanted to own that house.... But I fought the temptation away.... Oh, I inquired of course. The replies were discouraging. And once every year or so I drove by and stared sadly and even more sadly and brokenly

the House of the Black Burghardts stared back. Then all of a sudden somebody whose many names and places I do not know sent secret emissaries to me on a birthday...And they said by telegram: 'The House of the Black Burghardts is come home again—it is yours!' Whereat in great joy I celebrated another birthday and drew plans. And from its long hiding place I brought out an old black pair of tongs. Once my grandfather, and mayhap his, used them in the great fireplace of the House. Long years I have carried them tenderly over all the earth. The sister shovel, worn in holes, was lost. But when the old fireplace rises again from the dead on Egremont Plain, its dead eyes shall see not only the ghosts of Old Tom and his son Jack and his grandson Othello and His great grandson, me—but also the real presence of these iron tongs resting again in fire worship in the House of the Black Burghardts. (1928: 133–134)

There was one thing beyond owning his childhood home that always stuck with Du Bois, he wanted to be back in that place, reclaiming the small piece of Burghardt land that meant so much to him, that provided his claim to kinship and his New England identity. He was never able to make that happen. That fireplace is long gone, but it has always been a dream of mine to take this small detail of his life and use it to remember him at the site. It would be nearly impossible to recreate the house of the Black Burghardts at the Boyhood Homesite today. However, imagine if there was a representation of that central fireplace, tongs resting by its side. I think it would be like Du Bois was truly at home again.

I want a Black Feminist Archaeology to provide a lens through which to see the stories of Black women's lives, and to add another dimension to how we view American women, women and work, Black families and the legacy and realities of race and racism. Black Feminist Archaeology provides a method that helps us see those historically marginalized peoples that by their sheer identity are simply overlooked. To be overlooked as an integral component of the story of the United States is a fact that as a person of African descent I could no longer justify in archaeology (or history for that matter).

For, at the center of the lives of these women of the African Diaspora, we need to recognize their roles within their families, the amount of work they completed in their lives, the effort, the blood, sweat and tears and the contributions to the global community. It is why Zora Neale Hurston once called us the "mules of the world"; our burdens get heavier the longer we carry them in silence. We carry them for our people, as cultural bearers, but also as those who make it possible for capitalism to grow, disparities between the haves and have nots to widen, and acknowledgement of the physical and psychological effects of racism to continue. As cooks, domestics, wet nurses, laundresses, seamstresses, lovers and field hands, we became part of the reason it was possible to maintain a Victorian sensibility, a cult of domesticity, a Women's Suffrage Movement. It makes me sigh when I hear about the liberation of women, but know that my ancestors and my sisters in struggle were and are in a perpetual state of servitude. It is similar to the irony of the American revolution: at the same time as colonists were fighting for their independence, we (women and men) were held in bondage. How is this possible and why are these two events, these two philosophies, not compared, the irony of what this means for our country, the relationship between Black and White people, Black and White women, and Black women and Black men?

I ask these questions in the most abstract, yet personal way. Many of these ideas have not come from me, but they have also come from many, many days and evenings of talking to women in my family, in kitchens in places like Virginia, North Carolina, Tennessee, Mississippi, Louisiana, New York and Texas. They have been shaped and transformed by the words I have read by other people inside and outside of the academy. Through it all, I think I have gained so much from my work preparing for excavations as the W. E. B. Du Bois Boyhood Homesite in Great Barrington. I needed contextualization for this site, and this has not been easy. For more than eight decades Du Bois wrote about his life, education, liberation, Africa, African America, poverty, social justice, women's rights and beyond. Reading his words day after day, month after month, year after year, I begin to understand that I will not get it in a season or a semester; I have my lifetime to figure it out. However, I want to build the framework for this life work ahead, and that is where I see a Black Feminist Archaeology moving beyond my inner thoughts and dreams. I, too, want to lay those tongs down on the hearth of my mother and my mother's mother. And once again we will sing...

> *Do banna coba gene me, gene me!*
> *Do bana coba, gene me, gene me!*
> *Ben d'nuli, nuli, nuli, nuli, ben d'le...*

(Song sung by Du Bois's great-grandmother, meaning unknown)

References

Allen, Jafari. 2004. *Counterpoints. Black Masculinities, Sexuality, and Self-Making in Contemporary Cuba.* Ph. D. dissertation, Columbia University, New York. Ann Arbor, MI: University Microfilms.

Agbe-Davies, Anna. 2003. "Archaeology and the Black Experience. *Archaeology* 56(1):22.

———. 2010. "Concepts of community in pursuit of an inclusive archaeology." *The International Journal of Heritage Studies* 16(6):373–389.

Agorsah, Kofi. 1994. *Maroon Heritage: Archaeological, Ethnographic, and Historical Perspectives.* Jamaica: University of West Indies Press.

Allison, Penelope. 1999. *The Archaeology of Household Activities.* New York: Routledge.

Baker, Vernon. 1978. *Historical Archaeology at Black Lucy's Garden, Andover, Massachusetts: Ceramics From the Site of a Nineteenth Century Afro-American.* Papers of the Robert S. Peabody Foundation for Archaeology, Vol. 8, Phillips Academy, The Foundation, Andover, MA.

Barile, Kerri and Jamie Brandon (editors). 2004. *Household Chores and Household Choices: Theorizing the Domestic Sphere in Historical Archaeology.* Tuscaloosa: University of Alabama Press.

Battle, Whitney. 2004. *A Yard to Sweep: Race, Gender and the Enslaved Landscape.* Ph. D. dissertation, University of Texas, Austin. Ann Arbor, MI: University Microfilms.

Battle-Baptiste, Whitney. 2007a. "A Place of Our Own: Redefining the Enslaved Landscape at Andrew Jackson's Hermitage Plantation." In *Household Chores and Household Choices*, edited by Kerri Barile and Jamie Brandon, pp. 33–52. Tuscaloosa: University of Alabama Press.

———. 2007b. "The Other From Within: A Commentary." In *Past Meets Present: Archaeologists Partnering with Museum Curators, Teachers, and Community Groups*, edited by John Jameson and Sherene Baugher, pp. 101–106. New York: Springer.

———. 2010a. "Sweepin' Spirits: Power and Transformation on the Plantation Landscape." In *The Archaeology and Preservation of Gendered Landscapes*, edited by Sherene Baugher and Suzanne Spender-Wood, pp. 81–94. New York: Springer.

———. 2010b. "An Archaeologist Finds Her Voice: A Commentary." In *Handbook of Postcolonial Archaeology*, edited by Jane Lydon and Uzma Rizvi, pp. 387–392. World Archaeological Congress Research Handbooks in Archaeology, Volume 3. Walnut Creek, CA: Left Coast.

Beaudry, Mary. 1989. "Household Structure and the Archaeological Record: Examples from New World Historical Studies." In *Households and Communities*, edited by S. MacEachern, D. Archer and R. Garvin, pp. 84–92. Calgary, AB: University of Calgary Press.

———. 1993. *Documentary Archaeology in the New World*. Cambridge, UK: Cambridge University Press.

Beaudry, Mary and Stephen Mrozowski. 1989. "The Archaeology of Work and Home Life in Lowell, Massachusetts: An Interdisciplinary Study of the Boott Cotton Mills Corporation." *The Journal of the Society for Industrial Archaeology* 14(2):1–22.

Bell, Allison. 2008. "On the Politics and Possibilities for Operationalizing Vindicationist Historical Archaeologies." *Historical Archaeology*, 42(2):138–146.

Berlin, Ira. 1998. *Many Thousands Gone: The First Two Centuries of Slavery in North America*. Cambridge, MA: Harvard University Press.

Blakey, Michael. 1997. "Past Is Present: Comments on 'In the Realm of Politics: Prospects for Public Participation in African-American Plantation Archaeology.'" *Historical Archaeology*, 31(3):140–145.

Blassingame, John. 1979. *The Slave Community: Plantation Life in the Antebellum South*. New York: Oxford University Press.

Blier, Suzanne. 1995. *The Anatomy of Architecture: Ontology and Metaphor in Batammaliba Architectural Expression*. Cambridge, UK: University of Cambridge Press.

Bluestain, Melinda. 2010. Personal communication, Robert Peabody Museum of Archaeology, Andover, MA.

Bourdieau, Pierre. 1977. *Outline of a Theory of Practice*. Cambridge, UK: Cambridge University Press.

Brandon, Jamie. 2008a. "Disparate Diasporas and Vindicationist Archaeologies: Some Comments on Excavating America's Metaphor." *Historical Archaeology* 42(2):147–151.

———. 2008b. "History and Archaeology at Van Winkle's Mill: Recovering Lost Industrial and African-American Heritages in the Arkansas Ozarks." *Arkansas Historical Quarterly* 65(4):429–449.

Breeden, John. 1980. *Advice Among Masters: The Ideal in Slave Management in the Old South*. Westport, CT: Greenwood.

Brigance, Fred. 1975. *Historical Background of the First Hermitage*. Ladies' Hermitage Association and the Tennessee Bicentennial Commission, Hermitage, TN.

Brown, Barbara. 2010. Personal Communication, Lawrence, MA.

Brown, Kenneth. 1994. "Material Culture and Community Structure: The Slave and Tenant Community at Levi Jordan Plantation, 1848–1892." In *Working Toward Freedom: Slave Society and Domestic Economy in the American South*, edited by Larry Hudson, pp. 95–118. Rochester, NY: University of Rochester Press.

Brown, Kenneth and Doreen Cooper. 1990. "Structural Continuity in an African-American Slave and Tenant Community." *Historical Archaeology* (24)4:7–19.

Brumfiel, Elizabeth. 1991. "Weaving and Cooking: Women's Production in Aztec Mexico." In *Engendering Archaeology*, edited by Joan Gero and Margaret Conkey, pp. 224–254. New York: Wiley-Blackwell.

Bullen, Ripley and Adelaide Bullen. 1945. "Black Lucy's Garden." *Bulletin Massachusetts Archaeological Society* 6(2):17–28.

Burgess, Norma and Eurnestine Brown. 2000. *African American Woman: An Ecological Perspective*, New York: Falmer.

Bush, Barbara. 1990. *Slave Women in Caribbean Society, 1650–1838*. Bloomington: Indiana University Press.

Candelario, Ginetta. 2007. *Black Behind the Ears: Dominican Racial Identity from Museums to Beauty Shops*. Durham, NC: Duke University Press.

Carby, Hazel. 1987. *Reconstructing Womanhood: The Emergence of the Afro-American Woman Novelist*. New York: Oxford University Press.

Caldwell, Kia Lilly. 2006. *Negras in Brazil: Re-envisioning Black Women, Citizenship, and the Politics of Identity*. New Brunswick, NJ: Rutgers University Press.

Claassen, Cheryl. 1997. *Women in Prehistory: North America and Mesoamerica*. Philadelphia: University of Pennsylvania Press.

———. 1999. "Black and White Women at Irene Mound." In *Grit Tempered: Early Women Archaeologists in the Southeastern United States*, edited by Nancy M. White, Lynne P. Sullivan, and Rochelle A. Marrinan, pp. 92–114. Gainesville: University Press of Florida.

Clark, Mary Ann. 2005. *Where Men are Wives and Mother's Rule: Santeria Ritual Practices and Their Gender Implications*. Gainesville: University Press of Florida.

Cohen, Getzel and Martha Sharp Joukowsky. 2007. *Breaking Ground: Pioneering Women Archaeologists*. Ann Arbor: University of Michigan Press.

Collins, Patricia Hill. 2000. *Black Feminist Thought: Knowledge, Consciousness, and the Politics of Empowerment*. New York: Routledge.

———. 2006. *From Black Power to Hip Hop: Racism, Nationalism, and Feminism*. Philadelphia: Temple University Press.

Combahee River Collective. 1982. "A Black feminist statement." In *All the Women Are White, All the Blacks Are Men, But Some of Us Are Brave*, edited by Gloria T. Hull, Patricia Bell Scott and Barbara Smith, pp. 13–22. New York: Feminist.

Conkey, Margaret. 2007. "Questioning Theory: Is There a Gender of Theory in Archaeology?" *Journal of Archaeological Method & Theory* (14):285–310.

Crenshaw, Kimberlé Williams. 1989. "Demarginalizing the Intersection of Race and Sex: A Black Feminist Critique of Antidiscrimination Doctrine, Feminist Theory and Antiracist Politics." *University of Chicago Legal Forum*: 139–167.

Davis, Angela. 1981. *Women, Race, and Class*. New York: Vintage.

———. 2003. *Are Prisons Obsolete?* New York: Open Media.

Deagan, Kathleen and Darvie MacMahon. 1995. *Fort Mose: Colonial America's Black Fortress of Freedom*. Gainesville: University Press of Florida.

DeCorse, Christopher. 1999. "Oceans Apart: Africanist Perspectives on Diaspora Archaeology." In *'I, Too, Am America': Archaeological Studies of African-American Life*, edited by Theresa Singleton, pp. 132–158. Charlottesville: University of Virginia Press.

Deetz, James. 1996. *In Small Things Forgotten: An Archaeology of Early American Life.* New York: Anchor Books.

Delle, James. 1998. *An Archaeology of Social Space: Analyzing Coffee Plantations in Jamaica's Blue Mountains.* New York: Springer.

Dorris, Mary C. 1915. *Preservation of the Hermitage 1889-1915: Annals, History, and Stories, The Acquisition, Restoration, and Care of the Home of General Andrew Jackson by the Ladies' Hermitage Association for over a Quarter of a Century.* Nashville, TN: Mary C. Dorris.

Drake, St. Clair and Horace Cayton. 1993. *Black Metropolis: A Study of Negro Life in a Northern City.* Chicago: University of Chicago Press.

Du Bois, W. E. B. 1899. *The Philadelphia Negro: A Social Study. Together with a Special Report on Domestic Service,* by Isabel Eaton. Philadelphia: University of Pennsylvania Press.

———. 1928. "The House of the Black Burghardts." *The Crisis* 35(4):133–134.

———. 1968. *The Autobiography of W. E. B. Du Bois: A Soliloquy on Viewing My Life from the Last Decade of Its First Century.* New York: International Publishers.

———. 1971. "The Trade in Men." In *The Seventh Son: The Thought and Writings of W. E. B. Du Bois,* edited by Julius Lester, pp. 471–488. New York: Vintage Books.

———. 1986. *W. E. B. Du Bois: Writings: The Suppression of the African Slave-Trade/ The Souls of Black Folk/ Dusk of Dawn/ Essays and Articles.* Des Moines, IA: Library of America.

duCille, Ann. 1994. "The Occult of True Black Womanhood: Critical Demeanor and Black Feminist Studies." *Signs,* vol. 19(3):591–629.

Dzidzienyo, Anani and Suzanne Oboler. 2005. *Neither Enemies nor Friends: Latinos, Blacks, Afro-Latinos.* New York: Palgrave Macmillan.

Edwards, Ywone. 1998. "'Trash' Revisited: A Comparative Approach to Historical Descriptions and Archaeological Analyses of Slave Houses and Yards." In *Keep Your Head to the Sky, Interpreting African American Home Ground,* edited by Grey Gundaker, pp. 245–271. Charlottesville: University Press of Virginia.

Elkins, Stanley. 1976. *Slavery: A Problem in American Institutional and Intellectual Life.* Chicago: University Press of Chicago.

Epperson, Terrence. 1999. "Constructing Difference: The Social and Spatial Order of the Chesapeake Plantation." In *'I, Too, Am America':*

Archaeological Studies of African-American Life, edited by Theresa Singleton, pp. 159–172. Charlottesville: University of Virginia Press.

Eyerman, Ron. 2002. *Cultural Trauma: Slavery and the Formation of African-American Identity*. Cambridge, UK: Cambridge University Press.

Fairbanks, Charles. 1984. "The Plantation Archaeology of the Southeast Coast." *Historical Archaeology* 18(1):1–14.

Fanon, Franz. 1952. *Black Skin,White Masks*. New York: Grove.

Farmer, Paul. 2004. *Pathologies of Power: Health, Human Rights, and the New War on the Poor*. Berkeley: University of California Press.

Fennell, Christopher. 2007. *Crossroads and Cosmologies: Diasporas and Ethnogenesis in the New World*. Gainesville: University Press of Florida.

Ferguson, Leland. 1992. *Uncommon Ground: Archaeology and Early African America, 1650–1800*. Washington, D. C.: Smithsonian Institute Press.

Fesler, Garrett. 2004. "Living Arrangements among Enslaved Women and Men at an Early-Eighteenth-Century Virginia Quartering Site." In *Engendering African American Archaeology, A Southern Perspective*, edited by Jillian Galle and Amy Young, pp. 177–236. Knoxville: University of Tennessee Press.

Fox-Genovese, Elizabeth. 1988. *Within the Plantation Household: Black and White Women of the Old South*. Chapel Hill: University of North Carolina Press.

Franklin, Maria. 1997a. *Out of Site, Out of Mind: The Archaeology of an Enslaved Virginian Household, c. 1740–1778*. Ph. D. dissertation, University of California, Berkeley. Ann Arbor, MI: University Microfilms.

———. 1997b. "Why Are there so Few Black American Archaeologists?" *Antiquity* 71:799–801.

———. 1997c. "'Power to the People': Sociopolitics and the Archaeology of Black Americans." *Historical Archaeology* 31(3):36–50.

———. 2001. "A Black Feminist-Inspired Historical Archaeology?" *Journal of Social Archaeology* 1(1):108–125.

Franklin, Maria and Larry McKee. 2004. "African Diaspora Archaeologies: Present Insights and Expanding Discourses." *Historical Archaeology* 38(1):1–9.

Franklin, Maria and Robert Paynter. 2010. "Inequality and Archaeology." In *Voices in American Archaeology*, edited by Wendy Ashmore, Dorothy Lippert and Barbara Mills, pp. 94–130. Washington, D.C.: Society for American Archaeology Press.

Frazier, E. Franklin. 1940. *The Negro Family in the United States*. Chicago: University of Chicago Press.

Freidan, Betty. 1964. *The Feminine Mystique*. New York: Dell.

Frost, John. 1861. *Pictorial Biography of Andrew Jackson*. New York: Henry Bill.

Galle, Jillian and Larry McKee. 2000. *Summary Report on the First Hermitage Excavation*. The Ladies Hermitage Association, Hermitage. Hermitage,TN: Hermitage Museum.

Galle, Jillian and Amy Young. 2004. *Engendering African American Archaeology: A Southern Perspective*. Knoxville: University of Tennessee Press.

Gaspar, David and Darlene Clark Hine. 1996. *More than Chattel: Black Women and Slavery in the Americas*. Bloomington: Indiana University Press.

Genovese, Eugene. 1976. *Roll, Jordan, Roll: The World the Slaves Made*. New York: Vintage.

Gero, Joan and Margaret Conkey. 1991. *Engendering Archaeology: Women and Prehistory*. New York: Wiley-Blackwell.

Giddings, Paula. 1984. *When and Where I Enter: The Impact of Black Women on Race and Sex in America*. New York: Bantam Books.

Gilroy, Paul. 1993. *The Black Atlantic: Modernity and Double-Consciousness*. Cambridge, MA: Harvard University Press.

Glassie, Henry. 1975. *Folk Housing in Middle Virginia*. Knoxville: University of Tennessee Press.

Gomez, Michael. 1998. *Exchanging Our Country Marks: The Transformation of African Identities in the Colonial and Antebellum South*. Chapel Hill: University of North Carolina Press.

Gordon, Edmund T. 1998. *Disparate Diaspora: Identity and Politics in an African Nicaraguan Community*. Austin: University of Texas Press.

Gramsci, Antonio, Quintin Hoare and Geoffrey Nowell Smith. 1971. *Selections from the Prison Notebooks*. New York: International Publishers.

Gundaker, Grey. 1993. "Tradition and Innovation in African-American Yards." *African Arts* 26(2):58–71, 94–96.

Gutman, Herbert. 1977. *The Black Family in Slavery and Freedom, 1750–1925*. New York: Vintage Books.

Guy-Sheftall, Beverly. 1995. *Words of Fire: An Anthology of American Feminist Thought*. New York: New Press.

Hamilton, James. 1987. "This Old House: A Karen Ideal." In *Mirror and Metaphor: Material and Social Constructions of Reality,* edited by Daniel Ingersoll, Jr. and Gordon Bronitsky, pp. 247–276. Lanham, MD: University Press of America.

Harrison, Faye V. 1999. "Introduction: Expanding the Discourse on 'Race.'" *American Anthropologist* 100(3):609–631.

———. 2008. *Outsider Within: Reworking Anthropology in the Global Age.* Champaign: University of Illinois Press.

Hautaniemi, Susan. 1994. "Race, Gender and Health at the W. E. B. Du Bois Boyhood Homesite." *Bulletin of the Massachusetts Archaeological Society* 55(1):1–7.

Hays-Gilpin, Kelley and David Whitley. 1998. *Reader in Gender Archaeology.* Florence, KY: Psychology Press.

Heath, Barbara and Amber Bennett. 2000. "'The Little Spots allow'd them': The Archaeological Study of African American Yards." *Historical Archaeology* 34(2):38–55.

Herskovits, Melville. 1969. *Myth of the Negro Past.* Glouster, MA: Peter Smith.

Hinshaw, Jane. 1979. *The First Hermitage.* The Ladies' Hermitage Association, Hermitage, TN: Hermitage Museum.

hooks, bell. 1990. *Yearning: Race, Gender, and Cultural Politics.* Boston: South End.

———. 2000. *Feminist Theory: From Margin to Center.* Boston: South End.

Hopwood v. State of Texas. 1996. Hopwood v. State of Texas, 861 F. Supp. 551 - Dist. Court WD Texas 1994.

Horton, James Oliver. 1993. *Free People of Color: Inside the African American Community.* Washington, D. C.: Smithsonian Institute Press.

Hudson-Weems, Clenora. 2004a. *Africana Womanism: Reclaiming Ourselves,* 4th ed. Troy, MI: Bedford Publishers.

———. 2004b. *Africana Womanist Literary Theory.* Trenton, NJ: Africa World Press.

Hurston, Zora Neale. 1995. *Zora Neale Hurston: Folklore, Memoirs, and Other Writings: Mules and Men, Tell My Horse, Dust Tracks on a Road, Selected Articles,* edited by Cheryl Wall. Des Moines, IA: Library of America.

Jones, Alice. 1998. "Sacred Places and Holy Ground: West African Spiritualism at Stagville Plantation." In *Keep Your Head to the Sky, Interpreting African American Home Ground,* edited by Grey Gundaker, pp. 93–112. Charlottesville: University Press of Virginia.

Jones, Gayl. 1987. *Corregidora*. New York: Beacon.

Jones, H. Lawrencie. 1997. Personal Communication. Chesapeake, VA.

Jones, Jacqueline. 1985. *Labor of Love, Labor of Sorrow: Black Women, Work, and the Family, from Slavery to the Present*. New York: Basic Books.

Jones, Robbie. 2002. *The First Hermitage Historic Structures Report*. The Ladies' Hermitage Association, Hermitage, TN: Hermitage Museum.

Kelso, William. 1986. "Mulberry Row: Slave Life at Thomas Jefferson's Monticello." *Archaeology* 39(5):28–35.

King, Wilma. 1998. *Stolen Childhood: Slave Youth in Nineteenth-Century America*. Bloomington: Indiana University Press.

Kitwana, Bakari. 2003. *The Hip Hop Generation: Young Blacks and the Crisis in African American Culture*. New York: Basic Civitas Books.

Kuper, Adam. 1993. "The 'House' and Zulu Political Structure in the Nineteenth Century." *The Journal of African History* 34(3):469–479.

Kuwayama, Takami. 2004. *Native Anthropology: The Japanese Challenge to Western Academic Hegemony*. Victoria, Australia: Trans Pacific.

LaRoche, Cheryl and Michael Blakey. 1999. "Seizing Intellectual Power: The Dialogue at the New York African Burial Ground." *Historical Archaeology* 31:84–106.

Lemire, Elise. 2009. *Black Walden: Slavery and its Aftermath in Concord, Massachusetts*. Philadelphia: University of Pennsylvania Press.

Leone, Mark. 2005. *The Archaeology of Liberty in an American Capital: Excavations in Annapolis*. Berkeley: University of California Press.

Leone, Mark and Gladys-Marie Fry. 1999. "Conjuring in the Big House Kitchen: An Interpretation of African American Belief Systems Based on the Uses of Archaeology and Folklore Sources." *The Journal of American Folklore* 112(445):372–403.

Leone, Mark, Cheryl LaRoche and Jennifer Babiarz. 2005. "The Archaeology of Black Americans in Recent Times." *Annual Review of Anthropology* (34):575–598.

Lewis, David Levering. 1994. *W. E. B. Du Bois, 1868–1919: Biography of a Race*. New York: Holt Paperbacks.

Little, Barbara. 1994a. "'She Was...an Example to Her Sex': Possibilities for a Feminist Historical Archaeology." In *Historical Archaeology of the Chesapeake*, edited by Paul Shackel and Barbara Little, pp. 189–201. Washington, D.C.: Smithsonian Institution Press.

———. 1994b. "People with History: An Update on Historical Archaeology in the United States." *Journal of Archaeological Method and Theory* 1(1):5–40.

———. 2007. *Historical Archaeology: Why the Past Matters.* Walnut Creek, CA: Left Coast.

Little, Barbara and Paul Shackel. 2007. *Archaeology as a Tool of Civic Engagement.* Lanham, MD: AltaMira.

Little, Barbara and Larry Zimmerman. 2010. "In the Public Interest: Creating a More Activist, Civically Engaged Archaeology." In *Voices in American Archaeology*, edited by Wendy Ashmore, Dorothy Lippert and Barbara Mills, pp. 131–159. Washington, D.C.: Society for American Archaeology Press.

Litwack, Leon. 1965. *North of Slavery: The Negro in Free States, 1790–1860.* Chicago: University of Chicago Press.

Lorde, Audre. 1982. *Zami: A New Spelling of My Name —A Biomythography.* New York: The Crossing Press.

McClaurin, Irma. 2001. *Black Feminist Anthropology: Theory, Politics, Praxis, and Poetics.* New Brunswick, NJ: Rutgers University Press.

McDavid, Carol. 1997. "Descendants and Decisions and Power: The Public Interpretation of the Archaeology of the Levi Jordan Plantation." *Historical Archaeology* 31(3):114–131.

McKee, Larry. 1995. "The Earth is Their Witness." *The Sciences* 35(2):36–41.

———. 1994. "Commentary: Is it Futile to Try and Be Useful? Historical Archaeology and the African American Experience." *Historical Archaeology* 23:1–7.

Mack, Mark and Michael Blakey. 2004. "The New York African Burial Ground Project: Past Biases, Current Dilemmas, and Future Research Opportunities." *Historical Archaeology* 38(1):10–17.

Majewski, Teresita and Michael O'Brien. 1987. "The Use and Misuse of Nineteenth-Century English and American Ceramics in Archaeological Analysis." *Advances in Archaeological Method and Theory* 11:97–207.

Malone, Anne. 1992. *Sweet Chariot: Slave Family and Household Structure in Nineteenth-Century Louisiana.* Chapel Hill: University of North Carolina Press.

Marrinan, Rochelle. 1999. "Best Supporting Actress? The Contributions of Adelaide Bullen." In *Grit Tempered: Early Women Archaeologists in the Southeastern United States*, edited by Nancy White, Lynn Sullivan and Rochelle Marrinan, pp. 148–162. Gainesville: University Press of Florida.

Massey, Doreen. 1994. *Space, Place and Gender*. Minneapolis: University of Minnesota Press.

Matthews, Christy. 1997. "Where Do We Go from Here? Researching and Interpreting the African-American Experience." *Historical Archaeology* 31(3):107–113.

Melish, Joan. 1998. *Disowning Slavery: Gradual Emancipation and Race in New England, 1780–1860*. Ithaca, NY: Cornell University Press.

Mintz, Sidney and Richard Price. 1992. *The Birth of African-American Culture: An Anthropological Perspective*. Boston: Beacon.

Miller, George, Ann Smart Martin and Nancy Dickinson. 1994. "Changing Consumption Patterns: English Ceramics and the American Market from 1770–1840." In *Everyday Life in the Early Republic: 1789–1828*, edited by Catherine Hutching, pp. 219–249. Winterthur, DE: Henry Francis du Pont Winterthur Museum.

Moraga, Cherrie and Gloria Anzaldua. 1983. *This Bridge Called My Back: Writings by Radical Women of Color*. New York: Kitchen Table.

Morgan, Edmund. 2003. *American Slavery, American Freedom*. New York: W. W. Norton & Company.

Morgan, Joan. 2000. *When the Chickenheads Come Home to Roost: A Hip-Hop Feminist Breaks It Down*. New York: Simon & Schuster.

Morrison, Toni. 1987. *Beloved*. New York: Alfred A. Knopf.

———. 1993. *Playing in the Dark: Whiteness in the Literary Imagination*. New York: Vintage Books.

Morton, Patricia. 1991. *Disfigured Images: The Historical Assault on Afro-American Women*. Lexington, KY: Praeger Paperback.

Moynihan, Daniel P. 1965. The Negro Family: The Case for National Action. Office of Policy Planning and Research, United States Department of Labor.

Muller, Nancy Ladd. 2001. *W. E. B. Du Bois and the House of the Black Burghardts: Land, Family and African Americans in New England*. Ph.D. dissertation, University of Massachusetts, Amherst. Ann Arbor, MI: University Microfilms.

Mullins, Paul. 1999. *Race and Affluence: An Archaeology of African America and Consumer Culture*. New York: Springer.

———. 2008. "Excavating America's Metaphor: Race, Diaspora, and Vindicationist Archaeologies." *Historical Archaeology* 42(2):104–122.

National Poverty Center. 2010. The University of Michigan Gerald R. Ford School of Public Policy. U. S. Census Bureau and the National Poverty Center. www.census.gov/hhes/www/poverty.

Neal, Mark Anthony. 2002. *Soul Babies: Black Popular Culture and the Post-Soul Aesthetic*. New York: Routledge.

Netting, Robert, Richard Wilk and Eric Arnould. 1984. *Households: Comparative and Historical Studies of the Domestic Group*. Berkeley: University of California Press.

Ogundiran, Akinwumi and Toyin Falola. 2007. *Archaeology of Atlantic Africa and the African Diaspora*. Bloomington: Indiana University Press.

Orser, Charles. 1996. *A Historical Archaeology of the Modern World*. New York: Plenum.

———. 1998a. "Archaeology of the African Diaspora." *Annual Review of Anthropology*. 27:63–82.

———. 1998b. "The Challenge of Race to American Historical Archaeology." *American Anthropologist* 100(3):661–668.

Otto, John. 1984. *Cannon's Point Plantation, 1794–1860: Living Conditions and Status Patterns in the Old South*. Orlando, FL: Academic.

Painter, Nell Irvin. 1996. *Sojourner Truth: A Life, a Symbol*. New York: W. W. Norton & Company.

Palus, Matthew, Mark Leone and M. C. Cochran. 2006. "Critical Archaeology: Politics Past and Present." In *Historical Archaeology*, edited by Martin Hall and Stephen Silliman, pp. 84–104. New York: Blackwell.

Parton, James. 1850. *Remembering the Hermitage*. On file at the Hermitage Museum, Hermitage, TN.

Patterson, Tiffany and Robin D. G. Kelley. 2000. "Unfinished Migrations: Reflections on the African Diaspora and the Making of the Modern World." *African Studies Review Volume* 43(1):11–45.

Patten, Drake M. 1997. "Cheers of Protest? The Public, the Past, and the Parable of Learning." *Historical Archaeology* 31(3):132–139.

Patton, Venetria. 1999. *Women in Chains: The Legacy of Slavery in Black Women's Fiction*. Albany: State University of New York Press.

Paynter, Robert. 1990. "Afro-Americans in the Massachusetts Historical Landscape." In *The Politics of the Past*, edited by Peter Gathercole and David Lowenthal, pp. 49–62. London: Unwin Hyman.

————. 1992. "W. E. B. Du Bois and the Material World of African-Americans in Great Barrington, Massachusetts." *Critique of Anthropology* 12(3):277–291.

————. 1997. "Du Boisian Perspectives on Identities and Material Culture." *Anthropology Newsletter* 38(5):11.

————. 2000. "Historical Archaeology and the Post-Columbian World of North America." *Journal of Archaeological Research* 8(3):169–218.

————. 2001. "The Cult of Whiteness in Western New England." In *Race and the Archaeology of Identity*, edited by Charles Orser, pp. 125–142. Salt Lake City: University of Utah Press.

Paynter, Robert, Susan Hautaniemi, and Nancy Muller. 1994. "The Landscapes of the W. E. B. Du Bois Boyhood Homesite: An Agenda for an Archaeology of the Color Line." In *Race*, edited by S. Gregory and R. Sanjek, pp. 285–318. New Brunswick, NJ: Rutgers University Press.

Paynter, Robert et al. 2005. "The Burghardts of Great Barrington: The View from the W. E. B. Du Bois Boyhood Homesite." Paper presented at the 38th Annual Meeting of the Society for Historical and Underwater Archaeology, York, UK.

Perry, Warren. 1998. "Dimensions of Power in Swaziland Research: Coercion, Reflexivity, and Resistance." *Transforming Anthropology*, 7(1):2–14.

Perry, Warren and Michael Blakey. 1997. "Archaeology as Community Service: The African Burial Ground Project in New York City. *North American Dialogue* 2(1):45–51.

Perry, Warren and Robert Paynter. 1999. "Artifacts, Ethnicity, and Archaeology of African Americans." In *"I, Too, Am America": Archaeological Studies of African American Life*, edited by Theresa Singleton, pp. 299–310. Charlottesville: University Press of Virginia.

Perry, Warren and Janet Woodruff. 2003. "African Spiritual Practices in the Diaspora: Looking at Connecticut." Connecticut Historical Commission. Connecticut State Library, Hartford, CT.

Piper, Emilie and David Levinson. 2010. *One Minute a Free Woman: Elizabeth Freeman and the Struggle for Freedom.* Upper Housatonic Valley National Heritage Area/African American Heritage Trail.

Phillips, U. B. 1918. *American Negro Slavery: A Survey of the Supply, Employment and Control of Negro Labor as Determined by the Plantation Régime.* New York: D. Appleton and Company.

Pogue, Dennis and Esther White. 1991. "The Domestic Architecture of Slavery at George Washington's Mount Vernon." *Winterthur Portfolio* 37(1):3–22.

Potter, Parker. 1991. "What Is the Use of Plantation Archaeology?" *Historical Archaeology* 25(3):94–107.

———. 1994. *Public Archaeology in Annapolis: A Critical Approach to History in Maryland's Ancient City.* Washington, D. C.: Smithsonian Institution Press.

Posnansky, Merrick. 1999. "West African Reflections on African-American Archaeology." *'I, Too, Am America': Archaeological Studies of African-American Life,*pp. 21–38. Charlottesville: University of Virginia Press. .

Prince, Mary. 1998. *The History of Mary Prince, A West Indian Slave, Related by Herself: Revised Edition.* Ann Arbor: University of Michigan Press.

Robertson, Claire. 1996. "'Africa in to the Americas': Slavery and Women, the Family, and the Gender Division of Labor." In *More than Chattel: Black Women and Slavery in the Americas,* edited by David Gaspar and Darlene Clark Hine, pp. 3–42. Bloomington: Indiana University Press.

Raboteau, Albert. 1980. *Slave Religion: The "Invisible Institution" in the Antebellum South.* New York: Oxford University Press.

Remini, Robert. 1998a. *Andrew Jackson: The Course of American Empire, 1767–1821* (Volume 1). Baltimore: Johns Hopkins University Press.

———. 1998b. *Andrew Jackson: The Course of American Freedom, 1822–1832* (Volume 2). Baltimore: Johns Hopkins University Press.

Rotman, Deborah. 2009. *Historical Archaeology of Gendered Lives.* New York: Springer.

Rushdy, Ashraf H. A. 1999. *Neo-Slave Narratives: Studies in the Social Logic of a Literary Form.* New York: Oxford University Press.

Russell, Aaron. 1997. "Material Culture and African-American Spirituality at the Hermitage." *Historical Archaeology* (31)2:63–80.

Saitta, Dean. 2007. *The Archaeology of Collective Action.* Gainesville: University Press of Florida.

Samford, Patricia. 1995. "The Archaeology of African-American Slavery and Material Culture." *William and Mary Quarterly* 53(1):189–206.

Sánchez-Eppler, Karen. 1998. "Review: Ain't I a Symbol?" *American Quarterly* 50(1):149–157.

Shackel, Paul. 1993. *Personal Discipline and Material Culture: An Archaeology of Annapolis, Maryland, 1695–1870.* Knoxville: University of Tennessee Press.

———. 2010. *New Philadelphia: An Archaeology of Race in the Heartland.* Berkeley: University of California Press.

Schiffer, Michael. 1987. *Formation Processes of the Archaeological Record.* Salt Lake City: University of Utah Press.

Scott, James. 1990. *Domination and the Art of Resistance: Hidden Transcripts.* New Haven, CT: Yale University Press.

Siebert, Wilbur. 1936. *The Underground Railroad in Massachusetts.* Worcester, MA: American Antiquarian Society.

Singleton, Theresa (editor). 1999. *'I, Too, Am America': Archaeological Studies of African-American Life.* Charlottesville: University of Virginia Press.

Singleton, Theresa and Mark Bograd. 1995. *The Archaeology of the African Diaspora in the Americas.* Guides to Historical Literature 2. Tucson: Society for Historical Archaeology.

Smallwood, Stephanie. 2008. *Saltwater Slavery: A Middle Passage from Africa to American Diaspora.* Cambridge, MA: Harvard University Press.

Smedley, Audrey. 1998. American Anthropological Association's Official Statement on "Race." Executive Board of the American Anthropological Association, Washington, D. C. www.aaanet.org.

Smith, Samuel. 1976. *An Archaeological and Historical Assessment of the First Hermitage.* Nashville: Division of Archaeology, Tennessee Department of Conservation.

———. 1977. "Plantation Archaeology at the Hermitage: Some Suggested Patterns," *Tennessee Anthropologist* (2)2:152–163.

Spector, Janet. 1993. *What This Awl Means: Feminist Archaeology at a Wahpeton Dakota Village.* St. Paul: Minnesota Historical Society Press.

Spencer-Wood, Suzanne. 1991. "Toward an Historical Archaeology of Materialistic Domestic Reform." In *The Archaeology of Inequality*, edited by Randal McGuire and Robert Paynter, pp.231–286. New York: Basil Blackwell.

———. 2006. "Feminist Theory and Gender Research in Historical Archaeology." In *Handbook of Gender in Archaeology*, edited by Sarah Milledge Nelson, pp. 59–104. Walnut Creek, CA: AltaMira.

Spillers, Hortense. 2003. *Black, White, and in Color: Essays on American Literature.* Chicago: University of Chicago Press.

Spivak, Gayatri Chakravorty, Donna Landry and Gerald MacLean. 1995. *The Spivak Reader: Selected Works of Gayatri Chakravorty Spivak.* New York: Routledge.

Stack, Carol. 1974. *All Our Kin: Strategies for Survival in a Black Community*. New York: Basic Books.

Stampp, Kenneth. 1989. *Peculiar Institution: Slavery in the Antebellum South*. New York: Vintage Books.

Steady, Chioma. 1993. "Women of Africa and the African Diaspora: Linkages and Influences." In *Global Dimensions of the African Diaspora*, edited by Joseph Harris, pp. 167–188. Washington, D.C.: Howard University Press.

Stuckey, Sterling. 1988. *Slave Culture: Nationalist Theory and the Foundations of Black America*. New York: Oxford University Press.

Sweet, James. 2003. *Recreating Africa: Culture, Kinship, and Religion in the African-Portuguese World, 1441–1770*. Chapel Hill: University of North Carolina Press.

Thomas, Brian. 1995. *Community Among Enslaved African Americans on the Hermitage Plantation, 1820s–1850s*. Ph. D. dissertation, State University of New York, Binghampton. Ann Arbor, MI: University Microfilms.

———. 1998. "Power and Community: The Archaeology of Slavery at the Hermitage Plantation." *American Antiquity* 63(4):531–552.

Thompson, Robert Farris. 1984. *Flash of the Spirit: African and Afro-American Art and Philosophy*. New York: Random House.

Ulysse, Gina. 2008. *Downtown Ladies: Informal Commercial Importers, a Haitian Anthropologist and Self-Making in Jamaica*. Chicago: University of Chicago Press.

Vlach, John Michael. 1990. *The Afro-American Tradition in Decorative Arts*. Athens: University of Georgia Press.

———. 1993. *Back of the Big House: The Architecture of Plantation Slavery*. Chapel Hill: University Press of North Carolina.

Walker, Alice. 1983. *Searching for Our Mother's Garden: A Womanist Prose*. New York: Mariner Books.

Wall, Diana. 1994. *The Archaeology of Gender: Separating the Spheres in Urban America*. New York: Plenum.

Wallace, Michele. 1975. "A Black Feminist's Search for Sisterhood." *The Village Voice* 28:6–7.

———. 1990. *Invisibility Blues: From Pop to Theory*. New York: Verso Books.

———. 1999. *Black Macho and the Myth of the Superwoman*. New York: Verso Classics.

———. 2004. *Dark Designs and Visual Culture*. Durham, NC: Duke University Press.

Walsh, Lorena. 1997. *From Calabar to Carter's Grove: The History of a Virginia Slave Community*. Charlottesville: University Press of Virginia.

Weik, Terry. 1997. "The Archaeology of Maroon Societies in the Americas: Resistance, Cultural Continuity, and Transformation in the African Diaspora." *Historical Archaeology* 31(2):81–92.

White, Deborah Gray. 1999. *"Ar'n't I a Woman?": Female Slaves in the Plantation South*. New York: W. W. Norton & Company.

White, Nancy Marie. 1999. "Women in Southeastern U. S. Archaeology." In *Grit Tempered: Early Women Archaeologists in the Southeastern United States*, edited by Nancy White, Lynne Sullivan, and Rochelle Marrinan, pp. 1–24. Gainesville: University Press of Florida.

Wilk, Richard and Robert Netting. 1984. "Households : Changing Forms and Functions." In *Households: Comparative and Historical Studies of the Domestic Group*, edited by Richard Netting, Robert Wilk and E. Arnould, pp. 1–28. Berkeley: University of California Press.

Wilk, Richard and William Rathje. 1982. "Household Archaeology." *The American Behavioral Scientist* 25(6):617.

Wilkerson, Isabel. 2010. *The Warmth of Other Suns: The Epic Story of America's Great Migration*. New York: Random House.

Wilkie, Laurie. 1995. "Magic and Empowerment on the Plantation: An Archaeological Consideration of African-American World View." *Southwestern Archaeology* 14(2):136–148.

———. 2000. *Creating Freedom: Material Culture and African American Identity at Oakley Plantation, Louisiana, 1840–1950*. Baton Rouge: Louisiana State University Press.

———. 2003. *The Archaeology of Mothering: An African-American Midwife's Tale*. New York: Routledge.

Winter, Eugene. 2010. Personal Communication. Lawrence, Massachusetts.

Wright, Rita. 1991. "Women's Labor and Potter Production in Prehistory." In *Engendering Archaeology*, edited by Joan Gero and Margaret Conkey, pp. 194–223. New York: Wiley Blackwell.

———. 1996. *Gender and Archaeology*. Philadelphia: University of Pennsylvania Press.

Yamin, Rebecca and Katherine Metheny. 1996. *Landscape Archaeology: Reading and Interpreting the American Historical Landscape.* Knoxville: University of Tennessee Press.

Yentsch, Anne. 1994. *A Chesapeake Family and Their Slaves: A Study in Historical Archaeology.* Cambridge, UK: Cambridge University Press,.

Yellen, Jean Fagan. 1987. *Incidents in the Life of a Slave Girl, Written by Herself.* Cambridge, MA: Harvard University Press.

Young, Amy. 2003. "Gender and Landscape: A View from the Plantation Slave Community." In *Shared Spaces and Divided Places: Material Dimensions of Gender Relations and the American Historical Landscape,* edited by Deborah Rotman and Ellen-Rose Savulis, pp. 104–134. Knoxville: University of Tennessee Press.

———. 2004. "The Beginning and Future of African American Archaeology in Mississippi." *Historical Archaeology* 38:66–78.

Index

Activisim 20, 60

African American Studies 20, 65

African American 20, 21, 25, 27, 34, 35, 41, 44, 48, 50, 54, 55, 56, 57, 60, 61, 62, 65, 68, 72, 73, 74, 80, 91, 92, 94, 97, 98, 100, 102, 107, 111, 112, 113, 114, 115, 117, 122, 130, 131, 132, 141, 142, 143, 145, 146, 152, 153, 160, 162, 166, 167, 170

African American Christian systems, 55

African American Studies 20, 65

African descendant Community 21, 116

    descendant communities 20, 92, 167

African Diaspora Studies 20, 99

    African Diaspora Theory 54

African Traditional Systems 55

Africana Studies and Research Center 59, 70

Agbe-Davies, Anna 28

Allen, Jafari 97

American Anthropological Association, Statement on Race 22

Andover, Massachusetts 30, 112, 120, 121, 122

Anti-slavery 127, 130

Archaeologist 20, 21, 22, 23, 25, 27, 28, 29, 33, 34, 36, 40, 42, 49, 50, 53, 54, 70, 71, 76, 77, 80, 90, 93, 98, 99, 105, 106, 109,110, 112, 113, 116, 118, 122, 126, 129, 130, 131, 148, 153, 155, 159, 160, 164, 166, 167, 168

African American archaeology 30, 34, 54, 80, 111, 113, 114, 122

African Diaspora archaeology 54, 72, 94, 109, 159, 160, 167

Americanist archaeology 20, 25, 30, 69, 77, 112, 119, 131, 166

plantation archaeology 25, 54, 77, 98, 112

post-contact archaeology 20, 22, 28, 47, 86, 111

Andover, Massachusetts 30, 112, 120, 121, 122

Baker, Vernon 112, 116, 128

Black domestic sphere 40, 72, 160

see also captive African domestic sphere

Black cultural production 37, 48, 87, 91, 93, 100, 106

Black family 39, 40, 49, 51, 94, 100, 162

dysfunctional Black family 39

Black feminism 7, 30, 39, 54, 60, 61, 64, 65, 67, 147, 164

Combahee River Collective 39, 65

Black Feminist Archaeology 23, 29, 30, 36, 45, 51, 62, 66, 67, 69, 70, 71, 72, 77, 85, 87, 89, 91, 106, 110, 114, 133, 143, 147, 164, 165, 169, 171

Black matriarchal tradition, 49

Black women 8, 9, 31, 35, 36, 39, 40, 41, 42, 44, 45, 46, 50, 56, 57, 58, 59, 62, 63, 64, 65, 118, 143, 147, 148, 162, 169, 170

African American women 35, 56, 57, 60, 61, 62, 143

African descendant women 30, 36, 44, 45,57

black women's fiction 41, 42

black women writers 42

stereotypes 56, 58

as culture bearers 40, 143

as overbearing black woman 50

Boyce-Davies, Carole 60

Brazil 29, 30, 43, 63

Breedon, John 102

Bullen, Adelaide 30, 109, 111, 113, 119, 120

Bullen, Ripley 110, 120, 122, 128

Burghardts 48, 135, 137, 138, 139, 142, 158, 153, 154, 155, 157, 169

    Black Burghardts 135, 137, 138, 139, 142, 148, 154, 155, 157, 169

Burghardt Du Bois, Mary 137, 140, 142, 144

Burghardt, Lucinda 151

Burghardt, Othello 141

Burghardt, Thomas 150

Captive African kinship networks 49

Captive domestic sphere 41, 87, 88, 94

    captive African domestic sphere 41, 87, 88

Carby, Hazel 60

Christian, Barbara 44

Civil Rights Movement 58, 59, 63

Class 7, 8, 9, 20, 22, 24, 26, 27, 29, 30, 39, 47, 59, 61, 70, 97, 109, 110, 117, 122, 130, 138, 142, 144, 147, 149, 153, 154, 155, 159, 160, 164, 165, 166

    classism 24, 55, 62, 110

College of William & Mary 27

Collins, Patricia Hill 59, 61, 62, 63

Colonial Williamsburg Foundation 28, 33

    Department of Archaeological Research, 28

    see also Department of African American Interpretation and Presentations

Communitas 97

Complex household 49, 93, 100, 105, 107, 142, 168

Conkey, Margaret 47
    Engendering Archaeology 47
Cornell University 59, 60, 70, 120
Crenshaw, Kimberlé 60
Critical Race Theory 20, 29
Cuba 30, 146
Cultural landscape 71, 72, 86, 90, 100

Davis, Angela 34, 50
Department of African American Interpretation and Presentations 28
Dominant patriarchal gender ideology 47
Du Bois, Alfred 137
Du Bois, W. E. B., 34, 135, 136, 137, 138, 139, 141, 142, 144, 145, 146, 147, 149, 151, 152, 153, 154, 155, 156, 158, 161, 166, 169, 170
    Boyhood Homesite 30, 46, 135, 154, 155, 158, 160, 161, 165, 166, 168, 170
    The Philadelphia Negro 49
duCille, Ann 35, 60

Eastern Band Cherokee 26
Edwards-Ingram, Ywone 28, 98
Equal Rights Movement 47
    See also Women's Movement
Eurocentrism 50

The First Hermitage Site 75, 76, 80, 81, 83, 85, 86, 94, 95, 96, 97, 100, 101, 103, 104, 105, 106
    cooking pit 103, 104
    Jackson Farmhouse 76, 83, 84
    kitchen quarter 76, 83, 103, 104
    Mansion Backyard 81
    Triplex Quarters 89

Foster, Lucy 30, 47, 109, 111, 112, 113, 114, 116, 118, 122-132, 166

Franklin, Maria 27, 37, 38, 64, 84, 111, 112

Frazier, E. Franklin 49

    The Negro Family in the United States 49

Functional Plantation Model 85–86

Frost, John 78

Garvey, Marcus 34

gender, 7, 9, 20, 21, 22, 29, 30, 35, 36, 37, 38, 39, 40, 42, 45, 46, 47, 48, 55, 57, 58, 59, 61, 62, 64, 66, 70, 77, 89, 102, 104, 109, 111, 117, 118, 119, 120, 131, 132, 144, 145, 147, 155, 159, 164, 165, 166, 167

    gender power dynamics 47

    gender division 48

Gero, Joan 47

    Engendering Archaeology 47

Giddings, Paula 57

    When and Where I Enter 57

global community 25, 170

Great Barrington, Massachusetts 30, 135, 136, 137, 138, 139, 140, 142, 144, 145, 149, 150, 152, 154, 157, 158, 160, 166, 170

Habitus 85, 98

Haiti 30, 115

hand-me-downs 106, 117

Hermitage, Tennessee 28, 30

    The Hermitage, 73, 74, 75, 76, 77, 78, 79, 82, 83, 85, 89, 92, 102, 106, 107, 142, 145, 168

hip-hop generation 63, 65

historical narrative 39

Historically Black Colleges 26

homespace 94, 95, 96, 97, 99, 100, 101, 102, 103, 105, 106

hooks, bell 24, 61, 94, 95
Hopwood Decision 24

Intersectionality 20, 29, 70, 164
Irene Mound 68, 69, 120

Jackson, Andrew 30, 75, 77, 78, 79, 82, 83 84
    as Old Hickory 77
Jacobs, Harriet 40, 42
Jones, Gayl 19, 43, 46
    Corregidora 19, 43

Ladies' Hermitage Association 79
LaRoche, Cheryl 28, 130
Lordes, Audre 44, 163

Material culture 29, 30, 37, 71, 99, 106, 109, 117, 159, 167
McKee, Larry 33, 80
Mesoamerican site 47, 48
Mohanty, Chandra 60
Morrison, Toni 43, 46, 90
    Beloved 43
The Moynihan Report 50, 160
Mullins, Paul 22, 54, 55, 64
multiple family domestic social system 48

narrative tradition 29
Neal, Mark Anthony 63
The Negro Family, the Case for National Action 50
neo-slave narrative 44

Obama, Barack 23

Pan-Africanism 52, 55
Patriarchy 40, 51, 100
Patton, Venetria 42
Poverty 24, 50, 65, 72, 115, 117, 129, 130, 138, 153, 160, 166, 170
Prince, Mary 43
public schools 24

Race 55, 57, 58, 59, 60, 61, 62, 64, 68, 69, 70, 87, 88, 98, 109, 111, 115, 117, 118, 130, 132, 144, 146, 147, 149, 150, 154, 155, 158, 159, 160, 164, 165, 166, 167, 169
    racialization 23
    racism 22, 24, 26, 27, 28, 34, 53, 54, 55, 57, 58, 59, 61, 62, 63, 64, 65, 70, 94, 110, 112, 118, 169, 170
re-memory 46
Robertson, Claire 51
sister scholars 45
slavery 26, 27, 34, 42, 43, 44, 50, 51, 77, 89, 95, 98, 99, 105, 114, 117, 118, 121, 124, 131, 132, 143, 147, 162
social justice 31, 56, 64, 167, 168, 170
soul baby, 63
the South 24, 26, 27, 28, 75, 102, 115, 131, 144, 147, 152
Spillers, Hortense 60
Spivak, Gayatri Chakravorty 55
stakeholders 20, 21, 70, 145, 159
strong Black woman 40
Subaltern 55
    hegemonic notions of power 55
Sweet, James 50
    Recreating Africa 50

Tennessee American Revolution Bicentennial Commission 80
Trail of Tears 26

University of Massachusetts Amherst 21, 112, 154
University of Texas 24, 112, 135

Virginia State University 26
Vodou 55

Walker, Alice 38
Wallace, Michele 60
W. E. B. Du Bois Department of Afro-American Studies 154, 155, 160
W. E. B. Du Bois Center (University of Massachusetts Amherst) 161
Western New England 26
Williamsburg, Virginia 27, 28, 33, 111
Womanist 36, 37, 38, 45, 155
    Womanism 59
Women's Movement 23
Wylie, Alison 47

yardscape 90, 92, 96, 100, 102, 104
Yoruba 91
    see also Yoruba language
Yoruba language 55

About the Author

Whitney Battle-Baptiste is Assistant Professor of Anthropology at the University of Massachusetts, Amherst. A historical archaeologist of African and Cherokee descent, she has done fieldwork at Colonial Williamsburg, the Hermitage, the W. E. B DuBois Homesite, and other sites. She holds a Ph.D. from the University of Texas, Austin, and conducts research on plantations in the U.S. Southeast, the materiality of contemporary African American popular culture, and Black Feminist theory and its implications for archaeology.